Decorative Accents for the Garden

Shades Of Battenburg Lace

Decorative Accents for the Garden

by Emily Phillips

Sterling Publishing Co., Inc. New York
A Sterling/Chapelle Book

For Chapelle Ltd.

Owner
Jo Packham

Editor
Cherie Hanson

Staff
Malissa Boatwright • Sara Casperson • Rebecca Christensen • Holly Fuller
Sharon Ganske • Amber Hansen • Holly Hollingsworth • Susan Jorgensen
Kristin Kapp • Susan Laws • Amanda McPeck • Barbara Milburn
Pat Pearson • Jamie Pierce • Leslie Ridenour • Cindy Rooks • Edie Stockstill
Cindy Stoeckl • Ryanne Webster • Nancy Whitley

Photography
Kevin Dilley for Hazen Photography

Styling
Rebecca Christensen • Cherie Herrick • Jo Packham

If you have any questions or comments or would like information on specialty products featured in this book, please contact Chapelle, Ltd., Inc., PO Box 9252, Ogden, UT 84409; 801-621-2777;801-621-2788 (fax).

Library of Congress Cataloging-in-Publication Data

Phillips, Emily.
    Decorative accents for the garden / by Emily Phillips.
       p.   cm.
    "A Sterling/Chapelle book."
    Includes index.
    ISBN 0-8069-6122-8
    1. Handicraft.   2. Garden ornaments and furniture.   3. Woodwork.
I. Title.
TT157.P467   1996
745.5—dc20   95-45969
                                                  CIP

A Sterling/Chapelle Book

3   5   7   9   10   8   6   4   2

First paperback edition published in 1999 by
Sterling Publishing Company, Inc.
387 Park Avenue South, New York, N.Y. 10016
© 1996 by Chapelle Limited
Distributed in Canada by Sterling Publishing
℅ Canadian Manda Group, One Atlantic Avenue, Suite 105
Toronto, Ontario, Canada M6K 3E7
Distributed in Great Britain and Europe by Cassell PLC
Wellington House, 125 Strand, London WC2R 0BB, England
Distributed in Australia by Capricorn Link (Australia) Pty Ltd.
P.O. Box 6651, Baulkham Hills, Business Centre, NSW 2153, Australia
Printed in Hong Kong
All rights reserved

Sterling ISBN 0-8069-6122-8 Trade
0-8069-6123-6 Paper

Special Delivery

Illumination
61

Cultivation
75

Jubilation
127

CANDLESTICK
HOLDERS
LAWN TORCHES
LANTERNS
PATIO LIGHTS

PLANTERS
FLOWERPOTS
HOSE GUARDS
FENCE BORDERS
POOL STAKES

SWING SET
FOUNTAIN
GARDEN LADIES
SCARECROW
GARDEN COW

Preparation

Many of the projects in this book call for special techniques which are explained in this Preparation section. Referring to these general instructions will enable you to complete the projects more easily, efficiently, and produce pieces that will last through the years.

Tracing Patterns onto Wood, Cement, or Ceramic

Materials and tools you will need include tracing paper, transfer paper, pencil, photocopy machine and large-sized paper if necessary, and drafting tape.

- Lay a sheet of tracing paper on top of pattern and trace.

- If directions indicate enlarging a pattern, place pattern directly in a photocopy machine. Set the machine to percentage required and enlarge. If the enlarged pattern is on a grid, mark 1" grid lines on paper large enough to accommodate actual size pattern. Begin marking dots on 1" grid lines where the reduced pattern intersects the corresponding grid line. Connect the dots to finish pattern.

- Tape traced or photocopied pattern in place on the surface of the object to be cut or painted.

- Insert a piece of transfer paper between pattern and the object. Trace over pattern, transferring marks to object.

Because tracing paper is thin enough to see through, it allows the original pattern lines to be retraced easily. Transfer paper is coated on one side with graphite or chalk. When it is pressed by a pencil, it transfers the graphite or chalk to the surface under it. Since transfer paper is coated on only one side, make a small mark and determine if the correct side is down.

Transfer paper comes in a variety of colors, which is helpful when working on different colored backgrounds. For instance, black graphite works well on unfinished pine, but white or yellow would be easier to see on dark green surfaces. To reduce the amount of marks on the project, trace partial, or dashed, lines instead of the solid line.

Tracing Patterns onto Metal

Materials needed include tracing paper, tape, and a ballpoint pen or pencil

- Trace patterns onto tracing paper.

- Tape pattern over metal.

- Using a ballpoint pen or pencil, retrace the pattern onto the metal. For a deeper indentation, retrace several times.

Painting

Materials needed include acrylic paints, $1/4$" and 1" flat artist's brushes, a #2 round liner brush, a 2" utility paintbrush, and a sponge brush.

Artist's brushes are called flat or round; this refers to the shape of the metal part of the brush that holds the bristles onto the shaft. Brushes are numbered as well; the higher the number, the larger the brush. A size 10 flat, for instance, will be about an inch across; a size 5 is more like half an inch. A size 3 or #2 round is very small and is used for fine line work and details. Always use good-quality brushes and keep them clean.

Most of the painting on projects in this book are done in a simple style. After patterns have been traced and transferred, fill in with the background color first, then go back and paint fine detail lines, retracing them if necessary. It should be like coloring in a coloring book—just stay within the lines.

Most projects require primer or a base coat. This is usually a fairly good-sized area, so a larger brush makes for a faster job.

Acrylic paint cleans up with soap and water when wet. Be sure to clean brushes thoroughly with soap and water until the water runs clear. Never leave brushes standing in water overnight. It will soften the glue that holds the bristles and bend them out of shape.

It is always a good idea to use a drop cloth, old newspapers, or something to protect work areas. Acrylic paint will wipe right up off a nonporous surface, like tile or linoleum, or it will even peel off when dry. But acrylic paint on carpet will soak in immediately and probably not come completely clean. It is best in this case, if it is a small amount, to let the paint dry and cut it from the top of the carpet. Clothing too will be ruined by acrylic paint. It is recommended when working with acrylic paint to use a drop cloth and wear old clothes.

Painting on Ceramic Pots
In addition to materials and tools from Tracing Patterns and general Painting instructions, you will need elastic and reflective roof coating, acrylic primer/sealer, wood deck sealer.

Coat the inside of the pot with elastic and reflective roof coating as this will prevent moisture from seeping through the dirt to the outside of the pot. If the outside of the pot is to be completely painted with a design with no part of the original pot surface showing through, paint outside of pot and entire saucer with acrylic primer/sealer for surfaces. Let dry. Paint design on pot and saucer. Paint outside of pot, inside rim of pot and entire saucer with two coats of water seal for decks; let dry between coats. Do not apply sealer to any painted surface until it is completely dry, as smudging and smearing will result.

Painting on Metal
In addition to materials and tools from Tracing Patterns and general Painting instructions, you will need acrylic primer/sealer, varnish, and fine steel wool.

Many different types of latex paints are used in these projects for various effects. Copper paint and brass paint match the color of copper and brass almost perfectly. They are often used to cover soldering points. Acrylic paints are also used and can be applied with either brushes or sponges. Before applying acrylic paint, clean the surface of the metal with fine steel wool, then apply an acrylic primer/sealer for surfaces only on parts of project to be covered with paint. After applying acrylic paint, coat surface with two to three coats of varnish. Refer to Varnish instructions on page 10 before purchasing or applying varnish.

Painting on Wood
In addition to materials and tools from Tracing Patterns and general Paining instructions, you will need wood primer and wood deck sealer or varnish.

Paint inside and outside of wood projects with one coat of primer/sealer for wood. Let dry thoroughly. Apply paints according to manufacturer's directions for number of coats and temperature. If the paint is applied at the wrong temperature, the paint may bubble and peel over time. Coat inside and outside with two coats of water seal for decks. Varnish can be applied in place of the water seal, but make certain varnish is appropriate for weather conditions.

Antiquing and Washing
The materials and tools needed for antiquing are paint (burnt umber artist's oil paint for antiquing, white artist's oil paint for whitewashing, or specified color for washing), paint thinner, oil-based varnish, a 2" utility paintbrush, a bowl or other small container to mix paint, rags, and plastic gloves which are optional.
- Mix equal parts of artist's oil paint, paint thinner, and oil-based varnish. Most projects take about 2–4 tablespoons of each.

- Apply mixture to surface of project with a rag or 2" utility paintbrush.

- Wipe off excess before it sets up (usually within five minutes, depending on the temperature).

- The more stain left on, the more antiqued or whitewashed the project will look. If desired, more stain can be reapplied after a piece dries, but dried stain cannot be removed.

Dry Brush Painting
Some designs are painted using the dry brush technique. Simply pick up the paint with the paintbrush. Blot the brush on a scrap rag or piece of paper until brush is almost dry. Paint over surface to be dry-brushed.

Marbleizing
Paint project with a base coat or as indicated in specific instructions. The base coat for marbleizing is usually three to four different colors. To marbleize, dip a damp 1"-wide paintbrush into thinned paint; a 1:1 ratio of water to paint works well. Pick a point on edge of project and lay brush down. Pull brush along surface with a twisting, turning motion, making a vein. The twisting motion varies the thickness, and the turning makes a crooked, natural looking line. Some parts of the vein should have more paint than others. Veins in marble are mush like the branches of a tree— irregular, splitting, and often forming a Y-shape. Repeat using a #2 round liner paintbrush to make smaller veins.

Painting Small Dots
Some designs are made up of dots. Dots are, of course, small circles filled in and may be painted this way, but a simple technique is to dip the handle end of a paintbrush or similar-sized object, such as a pencil eraser, and use it like a stamp to make the dot.

Splatter Painting
This is a technique that uses a toothbrush. Dip the toothbrush bristles into the paint, and then run finger over the bristles to splatter-paint project. When the paints have dried, they are sealed with either a wood deck sealer or a lacquer finish, as specified in each project. In all cases, follow the manufacturer's instructions for paints and finishes.

Primers, Sealers & Varnishes
Elastic and Reflective Roof Coating
Because pots are made of porous material, it is a good idea to coat the inside of the pots with elastic and reflective roof coating. This will prevent moisture from seeping through the dirt to the outside of the pot.

Matte Spray

Clear matte finish spray is occasionally used to finish projects. The matte spray seals paints, patinas, and other antiquing methods. Matte spray will also delay the tarnishing process that occurs naturally on brass and copper. Check with local craft or paint store to make certain spray will be adequate for outdoor conditions.

Primer

Apply primer before painting. It is used to improve the application and adhesion of acrylic paints. Wood primer is available in two varieties, so check with a local paint store to determine which primer should be used for the project, the weather conditions, and the intended use of the project. Acrylic primer/sealer for surfaces is used to help paint adhere to slick or porous surfaces such as clay pots, wood, and metal. It also extends the life of projects exposed to various weather conditions.

Varnish

Spray varnish is easier to use than spread varnish, but it is more difficult to achieve an even coat. Although spray varnish is more expensive, it is the best choice to varnish items such as metal chair legs and ornate projects. Use a high-quality varnish as well as the appropriate type for each project and its intended uses. Check with a local paint store for recommendations and follow manufacturer's instructions carefully.

Wood Deck Sealer

After projects are completed, apply wood deck sealer to protect the crafted items from water and weather. The deck sealer is absorbed into the actual material of the project, whereas a varnish simply coats the surface. Wood deck sealer will protect painted or exposed surfaces against premature peeling or cracking.

Special Techniques

Découpaging

Materials need for découpaging are craft glue, or ready made découpage glue, water-base varnish, and an old paintbrush.

Combine one-part water and one-part craft glue, or use ready-made découpage glue. Using paintbrush, paint back of artwork with glue. Lay artwork on piece to be découpaged; press down with fingertips and remove any air bubbles. Brush several light coats of glue over artwork; let dry between coats. Apply several thin coats of water-base varnish to piece to protect it from water or weather.

Gold Leafing

Materials needed include reddish-brown acrylic or oil paint, spray or leafing adhesive, sheets of gold leafing, rags, and a small paintbrush.

- Unless already a reddish-brown color, paint pieces with a coat of reddish-brown acrylic paint. Allow to dry.

- Spray pieces with adhesive, allowing it to set a minute before proceeding.

- Apply the gold leaf, one sheet at a time. Brush gently with a dry paintbrush so that the gold leaf adheres to the surface. Remember that the first time the leaf touches the adhesive, it is permanent. If coverage is not as complete as desired, apply more gold leaf.

- Allow adhesive and leafing to dry completely, usually about 24 hours.

- If desired, brush leafing with a thin coat of burnt umber paint, then wipe with a clean rag. This will give leafing an aged appearance.

Woodworking

About Lumber

Dimensions for lumber are written with the thickness first and width second; for example, 1" x 12" means that the board is 1" thick and 12" wide. The next measurement tells how long the board is.

However, if you actually measure a board, you will find the dimensions are slightly smaller. This is a result of surfacing or planing at the lumber mill to remove the roughness of raw lumber. This makes no difference when using the lumber, so do not be alarmed if your boards do not "measure up."

About Tools for Woodworking

Most of the projects in this book are cut with a handheld electric jigsaw or scroll saw, which works well for 1"-thick pine. Some of the more advanced projects, such as the birdhouse picnic table, require a table saw or any type of saw that can cut through the thicker 2" x 4" pieces of wood.

Any project in this book that requires the use of power tools is an intermediate to advanced level project.

The following are some safety tips every woodworker should keep in mind:
- Read and understand all instructions that accompany power tools.

- Always wear safety glasses or goggles. Even when tools have blade guards, small pieces of wood sometimes splinter off.

- Use clamps, not hands, to hold the wood in place. Never allow hands to come near the cutting blade. It is recommended to keep both hands on top of the saw handle. Leaving hands on the wood could result in injury.

- Before working with a tool for the first time, ask for pointers and assistance from someone who is familiar with that tool.

Cutting Circles

When cutting circles or shapes in the middle of a board, first drill a hole in the part to be cut out. The hole needs to be large enough for the saw blade to fit into it (about $1/4$"). After the hole has been drilled, put blade into the hole and proceed just as on the edge of the board.

Jigsaw Basic Instructions

- After tracing the pattern onto the wood, clamp the board to a worktable with at least two large clamps. The pattern and wood should hang over the edge far enough that the wood can be cut but not so close that the worktable is cut. Cut approximately one foot at a time, moving and reclamping as the wood is cut. If too much of the wood hangs over the edge, too much vibration will result. Experiment with clamps and tools to determine what works best.

- Start on the outside edge of the board. Put saw feet on the board, but DO NOT let the blade touch the board. Turn the saw on and slowly ease the moving blade into the wood.

- Move the saw slowly, following the pattern lines. When going around corners and other tight turns, go very slowly and let the blade do the work.

- Make certain to replace blades when they become dull. A dull blade will break or cut very slowly.

- Be careful cutting through knots in the wood. They are very hard and difficult to cut through. Try to avoid putting cutting lines through knots wherever possible.

- When reaching a very tight turn, back up half an inch and make a second cut slightly outside the one being worked. When joining the second path to the original, a small piece of wood is cut out, allowing room to turn the blade and complete the cut.

- A fine wood-cutting blade usually achieves a clean cut, but sand rough edges when necessary.

Working with Metal

The following basic tools are needed for metal projects in this book: tin snips, an old pair of scissors, super glue, a soldering iron and solder, a small awl, a hammer, a hardwood hammering board, and needle-nose pliers.

Keeping these tools in a convenient location will facilitate your work and make it more enjoyable.

If painting metal, refer to Paining on Metal instructions on page 9. If varnishing metal, refer to Primers, Sealers and Varnishes instructions on page 10.

Cleaning Metal

Very fine steel wool is used for cleaning and polishing metal projects. It is a good idea to clean all projects with steel wool before antiquing or painting. This will remove any dirt or oil from your hands that could be present on the surface of the metal. For projects that are not antiqued or painted, gently polish the surface to restore the metal's original luster. Also use steel wool to clean a metal surface that has been tarnished from soldering.

Embossing

Embossing is indicated on the patterns by a thin, solid line. Emboss the pattern before cutting it out. Trace the embossing pattern onto a piece of tracing paper. Tape the paper in the appropriate place on the metal to be embossed. Place the metal on a stack of paper. Embossing can be done with a tin tool, a ballpoint pen, or a pencil. Simply trace the paper pattern onto the tin. Tracing the pattern on the metal right side up will produce indented embossing. Tracing the pattern on the metal wrong side up will create raised embossing. Tracing the pattern several times will create a deeper line and make the detail stand out more. Wipe the metal with a soft cloth to remove pen or pencil marks. A dry ballpoint pen also works well, since it will not leave any ink behind.

Soldering

Resin core solder is used in all projects requiring solder.

All soldering must be done before antiquing, painting, or finishing. It is recommended that a face mask is used while soldering to avoid breathing in lethal fumes.

Use a soldering iron instead of a soldering gun. A soldering iron is easier to control. Touch the iron to the spot on the metal to be soldered, then touch the solder to the hot spot on the metal. If this is the first time using a soldering iron, practice on scraps. A little solder goes a long way. If a mistake is made, touch the iron to the solder. The heat will melt the solder again and allow removal of it. The soldering spot can be covered up with a variety of metallic paints that will blend with the metal almost perfectly. Soldering may cause the metal to tarnish. If this occurs, use fine steel wool to gently clean the tarnished spot.

Inspiration

Barometer, Clock & Thermometer

Materials for One

One 18" x 30" piece of 3/4"-thick wood
Two hinges
Small wooden knob
Wood primer
Wood deck sealer
Découpage glue
Wood glue
Paintbrushes
Hammer and nails
Pocketknife
Saw
Color photocopy machine
For additional supplies, see specific instructions.

Instructions

1. Cut wood pieces according to diagram. Attach hinges to top and bottom on right side of doorway and top and bottom on right side of door. Glue doorknob to front of door. Nail house frame to center of base.

2. With pocketknife, whittle scallops along the bottom of one long side on each roof piece. Miter the inside edge of each of the roof pieces so that they will pitch over house top. Nail in place.

3. Paint back piece white, and attach to back of house covering doorway. Finish in one of the following designs:

BAROMETER

Paint wood with primer. When dry, paint entire house with **white acrylic paint**. Thin **rust acrylic paint** with water and paint stripes on front of house. Thin **golden brown acrylic paint** with water and wash roof.

Using a photocopy machine, enlarge anchor art on page 16 to 135%, and découpage above doorway. Dry-brush a scallop pattern on roof with **white acrylic paint**. Paint **one small pot** with **sky blue acrylic paint** and **one small pot** with **white acrylic paint**.

Using a color photocopy machine, enlarge life preserver art on opposite page 135%. Cut art to fit inside of doorway, and découpage. When dry, paint project with deck sealer; let dry. Attach a **7"-tall barometer** to inside of back wall, following manufacturer's instructions. Glue **pots** to ledge inside doorway.

CLOCK

Paint wood with primer. When dry, paint house with **blue-gray acrylic paint**. Dry-brush paint scallops with **light blue** and **white acrylic paints**. Paint freehand star shapes randomly on house with **gold acrylic paint**.

Using a color photocopy machine, enlarge lighthouse art on opposite page 135%. Cut art to fit inside of doorway. When dry, paint project with deck sealer. Let dry. Attach a **3½"-diameter clock** to inside of back wall, following manufacturer's instructions.

THERMOMETER

Paint wood with primer. When dry, paint entire house with **white acrylic paint**. Thin **pale yellow acrylic paint** with water, and wash over all surfaces, except roof. Thin **medium blue acrylic paint** with water, and wash over roof. Dry-brush paint scallops on roof with **pale yellow**.

Using a color photocopy machine, enlarge the sailboat and starfish art on page 16 to 135%. Cut out starfish, and découpage above doorway. Repeat with sailboat on inside of door. When dry, paint project with deck sealer. Let dry. Attach a **7"-tall thermometer** to inside of back wall, following manufacturer's instructions.

DIAGRAM

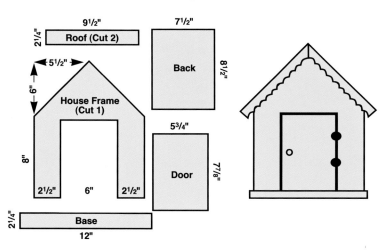

LIFE PRESERVER ART

LIGHTHOUSE ART

ENLARGE ART 135%

15

ENLARGE ART 135%

Beaded Angelic Wind Chimes

Beaded Angelic Wind Chimes

Fishing-Pole Wind Chimes

Materials

One gold wire angel (model is 9" tall)
Five 1" bells
One tiny bell
Approximately 50 beads in various shapes and golden-brown colors
Approximately 150 gold 4mm beads
4 yards of thin gold wire
Fishing line

Instructions

1. Cut a 20" length of gold wire. Twist one end onto one side of wings. Thread assorted beads across wire, twisting and wrapping to other side of wings. Repeat with two diagonal rows down angel's dress; see photo.

2. Cut five 12" lengths of fishing line. Thread a bell onto each length and tie in center. For first row, thread thirteen 4mm beads onto doubled line, then add an assorted bead and finish with a 4mm bead. Tie onto bottom of angel's dress about 1" in from left side. Trim excess fishing line. Create four more rows, adding five additional 4mm beads each time. Space rows evenly along bottom of angel's dress.

3. Make a loop with fishing line and tie to top of angel. Tie on an assorted bead and then the tiny bell.

Materials

Fishing equipment: small reel; end guide; line guide; and pop gear, consisting of five lures in assorted sizes, troll weight, swivel, five small sinkers, and fishing line
18" narrow tree branch
6" fat tree branch
Twine
Wood glue
Hot glue gun and glue sticks
Fine-grain sandpaper
Wire cutters
Drill

Instructions

1. Drill a hole in one end of 6" branch large enough to insert widest end of 18" branch. With wood glue, attach 18" branch into 6" branch; let glue set. Sand pole as necessary.

2. Hot-glue reel onto pole handle, line guide in center, and end guide at top, making sure they line up straight. Wrap twine around reel and center guide; hot-glue in place.

3. With wire cutters, cut off end weight from troll. Drill holes evenly around edges to attach each of the five lures.

4. To make chimes, cut wires between lures, leaving crimped clamp at one end, cutting wires at varying lengths: largest lure, longest wire; smallest lure, shortest wire. Bend wire down 1/2" at cut end. Hang lures from holes in troll from smallest to largest. Crimp one sinker at top of each wire.

5. Thread fishing line through guides and wind as much onto reel as desired. Cut five 18" lengths of line. Tie one piece of line into each hole on troll. Pull all lines up, make a 1" loop, and tie a tight overhand knot. Cut ends. Tie swivel onto line at end of pole. Open swivel and attach chimes.

seeds

Play Me A Garden Tune

Materials

One 4$^{1}/_{2}$"-diameter clay pot
Five miniature garden tools
Two 1"-diameter green wooden beads
One $^{1}/_{2}$"-diameter natural wooden bead
One 1"-diameter button
One star-shaped concho
Aluminum or tin scrap
8" of heavy wire
Fishing line
Light green, dark green, orange, purple, red, terra-cotta,
    violet, and white acrylic paints
Fine-tip permanent black marker
Acrylic primer/sealer
Matte spray sealer
Paintbrushes
Hot glue gun and glue sticks
Tin snips or old scissors
Photocopy machine

Instructions

1. Paint inside and outside of pot with acrylic primer and let dry. Using photo-copy machine, enlarge garden chimes patterns 165%. Paint vegetable pattern around pot. When dry, draw detail with black marker. Let dry. Spray with matte sealer.

2. Paint wooden handles of garden tools terra-cotta. When dry, spray with matte sealer.

3. Cut a 1$^{3}/_{4}$" x 2$^{1}/_{2}$" rectangle from aluminum or tin. Paint both sides with primer and let dry. Paint both sides white. Let dry. Paint carrot design and write "Seeds" with permanent black marker on each side. When dry, spray with matte sealer.

4. Make a loop in one end of heavy wire. Thread other end through wooden bead and then through hole in bottom of pot. Twist wire on inside.

ENLARGE PATTERNS 165%.

5. Tie a 5" length of fishing line onto inside wire. Thread other end through button and then through center of concho. Secure.

6. Cut five varying lengths of fishing line. Tie one end of each line around concho. Hot-glue other ends to each garden tool. Cut a longer length of fishing line and secure in center of concho. Thread remaining beads onto line and secure halfway down. Poke a hole through top center of "Seeds" rectangle and thread onto fishing line. Tie off.

Sunflower-Pot Wind Chimes

Materials

One 6"-diameter clay pot
Five 1³/4"-diameter clay pots
Three 1"-diameter colorful wooden beads
Five ³/4"-diameter colorful wooden beads
Two yards of ¹/4"-diameter twine
Fishing line
8" of heavy wire
Black, blue, brown, gold, green, orange, red, tan, and white
    acrylic paints
Acrylic primer/sealer
Wood deck sealer
Paintbrushes
Photocopy machine

Instructions

1. Paint all pots with acrylic primer and let dry. Excluding rims, paint outside of large pot and two of the small pots with a base coat of blue; paint remaining two pots with a base coat of red. Using a photocopy machine, enlarge and reduce sunflower pattern to fit each pot. Transfer patterns to pots and paint. When dry, paint with deck sealer.

2. Cut an 8" length of twine and tie a loop in top. Thread two 1" wooden beads onto twine. Place other end of twine through hole in bottom of large pot and slip on another 1" bead. Tie knot securely.

3. Cut 8", 9", 10", 11", and 12" lengths of twine. Secure one end of each piece of twine around knot inside large pot. Thread other ends of twine through small pots and tie a secure knot.

4. Thread fishing line through ³/4" beads, and tie around knot in center of each small pot. Wrap wire through top loop for hanger.

SUNFLOWER PATTERN

**ENLARGE
PATTERN
TO FIT
EACH POT**

Angels Know The Way Home

ANGEL PATTERN

ENLARGE PATTERN 165%

Materials

10" x 6" piece of $^3/_4$"-thick wood
2" wooden heart
$^3/_4$"-square wooden block
16" length of $^1/_4$"-square dowel
$^3/_4$" wooden letters: N, S, E, and W
16 small copper beads
Two tube-shaped decorative beads
13" of small chain
Three small eye screws
Fishing line
Medium blue, dark blue, and copper acrylic paints
Acrylic primer/sealer
Wood deck sealer
Wood glue
Fine-grain sandpaper
Paintbrushes
Awl
Drill with $^1/_8$" and $^1/_4$" bits
Scroll saw
Photocopy machine

Instructions

1. Using a photocopy machine, enlarge angel pattern 165%. Transfer pattern onto wood and cut out. Sand edges.

2. With $^1/_4$" bit, drill a hole about $^1/_4$" deep on four sides of block. With $^1/_8$" bit, drill a hole completely through top to bottom.

3. Cut dowel into four 4" pieces, and glue one piece into each side hole in block. Glue letters onto ends of dowels in appropriate positions.

4. With awl, make a hole in top and bottom of wooden angel and in top of heart. Insert eye screws.

5. Paint all wood pieces with acrylic primer. When dry, paint medium blue. Highlight with dark blue and copper by tapping paintbrush around outlines.

6. Hook chain to top eye screw. Paint chain and eye screws copper.

7. Tie fishing line onto eye screw on bottom of angel. Layer four copper beads, one decorative bead, four copper beads, wooden block, four copper beads, decorative bead, four copper beads, and heart. Tie off line securely and trim excess.

8. Coat entire project with deck sealer.

Tweet, Tweet, Place Your Feet

Materials

Rectangular cement blocks
Black, blue, green, purple, red, and yellow enamel paints
Weatherproof clear sealer
3" x 2" sponge
Paintbrushes
Photocopy machine

Instructions

1. Using a photocopy machine, enlarge pattern to fit cement block. Transfer bird pattern onto cement block. Paint bird portion as desired and referring to photo; do not paint leaves.

2. Cut sponge into a leaf shape, referring to pattern. Dip into green paint and blot off excess. Print leafs onto block.

3. Paint beak, legs, and dots yellow. Paint eye black. Let dry.

4. Coat blocks with weatherproof sealer.

BIRD GARDEN STONES PATTERN

ENLARGE PATTERN TO FIT BLOCK

Sun-Kissed Garden Stone

Materials

Red cement block
Wooden sun cutout (to fit top of block)
Ready-to-use mortar
Red cement color
Concrete bonder
Cement sealer
Rubber gloves
Stir stick
Old paintbrush

Instructions

1. Glue wooden sun in center of cement block with concrete bonder. Let dry.

2. Mix mortar, water, and red cement color until medium paste consistency. Apply a thin coat of mortar over and around sun, using finger to press out detail and smooth out bumps. Use pointed object to form face after mortar has set up a bit. Let set until hard, then apply cement sealer.

Any wooden shapes and cement colors can be used as shown on page 6. Try pressing marbles, seashells or other momentos into mortar as well.

Garden-Wall Memo Board

Materials

14$\frac{1}{2}$"-square wooden frame with 3" sides
14$\frac{1}{2}$"-square piece of cork board
1$\frac{1}{2}$" x 11$\frac{1}{2}$" piece of lattice
14" x 5" piece of balsa wood
5" length of $\frac{1}{8}$"-diameter wood dowel
Two $\frac{1}{4}$" x 1" x 3$\frac{3}{8}$" pieces of wood
Two miniature garden tools
Small birdhouse
Four 1$\frac{1}{2}$" clay pots
One 2" metal bucket (or wooden bucket painted silver)
Assorted flowers and vines
Miniature vegetable
Eucalyptus sprigs
Moss
Five squares of sculpting clay
Two small pieces of foam
Snow-texturizing medium
Brown, gold, dark gray, light gray, dark green, and rust
    acrylic paints
Acrylic primer/sealer
Wood deck sealer
Multipurpose cement glue
Paintbrushes
Pencil
Old toothbrush
Craft knife
Tin snips
Hammer and four small nails
Drill with $\frac{1}{8}$" bit
Saw

Instructions

1. Coat all pieces of wood, pots, and bucket with acrylic primer; let dry. Paint all edges of frame light gray; let dry.

2. With craft knife, cut balsa wood into 1" x 2" pieces. Paint the pieces rust. Let dry. Using a toothbrush, splatter-paint pieces with dark green, gold, and brown paints.

3. With saw, cut away a portion of three 1$\frac{1}{2}$" pots. Note: Cutting away about a fourth of the pots on the back sides will give them a flat surface for mounting.

4. With tin snips, cut away a portion of the bucket, as in Step 3.

5. Drill a hole in the bottom of birdhouse and also in the right center of one 3$\frac{3}{8}$" piece of wood.

6. Thin light gray paint with water, and wash both 3$\frac{3}{8}$" pieces of wood and the lattice piece. Thin gold paint with water, and wash handles of miniature garden tools and dowel. Thin brown paint with water, and wash birdhouse. Repeat with dark green paint for the roof.

7. Knead sculpting clay together, and roll out to about 12". Flatten to fit the width of frame. With pencil, draw deep lines into clay to form "rock wall." Bake, following manufacturer's instructions.

8. Paint clay wall with light gray, dark gray, and gold by mixing all colors onto one paintbrush and swirling onto surface.

9. Mix light gray paint with snow texturizing, and apply to top and sides of frame, stopping 3" up from bottom. Press balsa pieces in place as you work. Note: Some of the balsa "bricks" may need to be trimmed to fit. Let dry.

10. Glue clay wall onto bottom of frame with multipurpose cement glue. Glue lattice trellis to bricks on right side of frame.

11. Glue dowel into bottom of birdhouse, and glue the other end into the hole in the 3$\frac{3}{8}$" piece of wood. Glue uncut pot onto wood. Glue birdhouse and shelf to trellis. Stack three cut pots in right corner of frame and glue. Hammer four small nails horizontally across the flat side of remaining wood piece to act as "garden tool hangers." Glue to left side of frame about 4" down from top. Coat all pieces with deck sealer; let dry.

12. Add a vegetable to top pot. Glue vine up around trellis. Add a small piece of foam inside uncut pot and glue in flowers and vine.

13. Glue bucket to left corner of frame. Add a small piece of foam, and glue flowers and eucalyptus sprigs into bucket. Hang garden tools and glue down handles. Glue moss around bucket and pots. Cut cork board to fit inside of frame, and glue in place.

A Summer's Garden Fairy

Materials

4¹/₂" length of ¹/₂"-diameter wooden dowel
1¹/₄"-diameter round bead with ¹/₂" hole
30" of 16-gauge wire
Two purple silk mums in full bloom
Two purple silk mum buds
Small bunch of tiny purple flowers
Small amount of moss
4" x 45" piece of fleece
10 yards of light peach 7mm silk ribbon
18" of green 4mm silk ribbon
2 yards of green pearl cotton thread
Fishing line
Light peach acrylic paint
Silver glitter spray
Paintbrushes
Hot glue gun and glue sticks
Wire cutters
Drill with ³/₃₂" bit

Instructions

1. Mark ³/₈" up from one end of dowel, and drill hole through sides for leg wires. Mark ³/₄" down from opposite end of dowel, and drill hole through sides for arm wires. Cut wire into one 10" piece and one 20" piece. Insert longest wire through bottom hole, and bend down for legs. Insert shorter wire through top hole, and bend down and forward for arms.

2. Paint round bead with light peach paint, and glue to top of dowel. Glue moss on top of bead for hair.

3. Cut fleece into four 1" x 45" strips. Starting at neck, glue fleece to back of dowel and wrap around chest and arms. Repeat for waist and legs.

4. Cut light peach silk ribbon into 2-yard lengths. Cut four 1" pieces of light peach ribbon, and glue one piece to ends of arms and legs. Starting at neck, glue light peach ribbon to back of dowel and wrap snugly to cover fleece. Continue until completely covered. Glue ends.

5. Take silk flowers apart. Layer petals for skirt and around neck; hot-glue in place. Use bud petals for hat and under skirt. Use green leaves around neck. Use calyx of flower for cap.

6. For shoes, cut green thread in half and tie around ankles. Crisscross green pearl cotton thread to bottom of toes. Glue small flower bunches to toes.

7. Tie green silk ribbon around waist. Spray lightly with silver glitter, and suspend with fishing line.

Turn an ordinary wooden crate into a unique shelf onto which to hang the Garden Fairy or place flowerpots. Simply paint the bottom of the wooden crate a bright color, and coat with wood deck sealer.

Adoration

Ode To A Trellis Rose

Materials

16" x 60" piece of $^3/8$"-wide wood
12" x 36" piece of $^3/4$"-wide wood
Two 2"-long wood screws
Three screw hooks
Floral wrapping paper
Assorted jewels to match floral print
Black, cream, green, leaf-green, and light green acrylic paints
Wood primer
Wood deck sealer
Découpage glue
Industrial-strength glue
Paintbrushes
Hammer and nails
Saw
Photocopy machine

Instructions

1. Cut the following lengths from $^3/8$"-wide wood (all are $1^1/4$" wide): two 12", two $18^7/8$", six $22^1/4$", two $47^1/2$". From $^3/4$"-wide wood, cut one 32" x $1^1/2$" piece for center brace. For planter box, cut the following pieces from $^3/4$"-wide wood: one $3^1/8$" x $10^3/8$" piece for bottom, one $5^1/2$" x 12" piece for back, and two $3^1/2$" x $5^1/2$" pieces for sides; cut front piece according to diagram.

2. For planter box, nail the trellis slats together as in diagram, placing the vertical slats in the back and the horizontal slats in front. Nail the brace onto the back in the center of the second slat and running down to the last slat.

3. Nail side pieces between front and back pieces. Drop bottom inside box and secure with nails. Paint all wood with wood primer. When dry, paint trellis and inside of planter box light green.

4. Découpage planter box with floral paper. When completely dry, apply deck sealer. With industrial-strength glue, attach jewels randomly throughout floral pattern.

5. Using a photocopy machine, enlarge leaf pattern as desired to fit trellis. Transfer pattern onto trellis. Paint some leaves leaf-green and some cream. Highlight with light green and green. When completely dry, outline leaves and detail with a fine-tip paintbrush and black paint. When dry, apply deck sealer.

6. Attach planter box to trellis with wood screws. Screw two hooks on each end of top slat and one hook in center of second slat.

DIAGRAMS

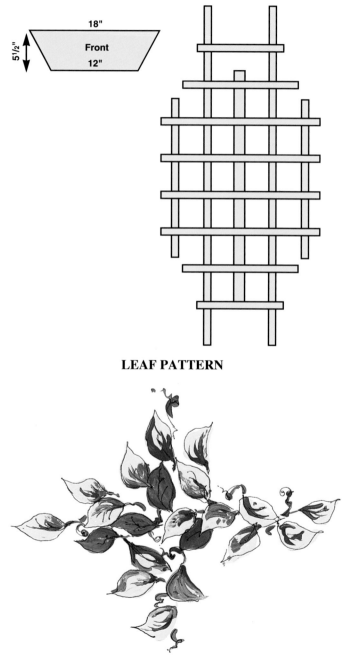

LEAF PATTERN

ENLARGE PATTERN AS DESIRED

The Shape Of Things To Grow

Materials

Willow branches (1" diameter for base structure,
    $1/2$" diameter for design)
Hammer and nails
Pruning shears

Instructions

The amounts and lengths of willows will be determined by the size of trellis desired. Model is $6^1/2$ feet high and $2^1/2$ feet wide.

1. Create a ladder-type base by placing two tall branches desired-width apart and nailing shorter branches horizontally across at various intervals. Note: Better balance will be achieved if width is smaller at bottom than top.

2. To create curved branches, soak in warm water until pliable. Nail willows in desired shape while soft.

TRELLIS DIAGRAM

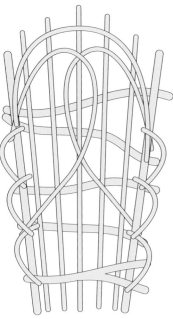

Shutter Screens To Store & Stack

Mother Nature's Garden Cafe

Materials

Three wooden shutters
Four hinges with hardware
Hunter-green latex paint
Wood primer
Fine-grain sandpaper
Paintbrushes

Instructions

1. Paint shutters with wood primer. Let dry.

2. Paint shutters with hunter-green latex paint. Let dry.

3. Sand shutters to create a distressed look.

4. Assemble shutters to form a standing screen. Tuck seed packets into slats, and hang garden tools as desired.

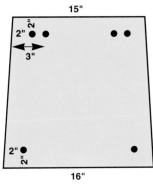*ang on garden wall near potting table, and use as organizer for tools, seed packets, and more.*

Materials

16" square of $3/4$" plywood
24"-diameter circle of 1" plywood
1"-diameter straight birch tree branches: two 24" lengths and six 16" lengths
Two 30" x 22" pieces of bark
Six 20" lengths of $3/4$" x 1" wood
Sheet moss
24 wood screws, $2^{1}/4$" long
Wood glue
Clamps
Saw
Drill with screwdriver bit

Instructions

For decorative purposes only. Photo on page 6.

1. Cut 16" plywood square, according to diagram, forming seat; drill holes where indicated. Predrill holes into one end of the 24" branches and into four of the 16" branches. On the 15" edge of the seat, screw two wood screws down from the top through the two outside holes. Attach 24" branches to seat with wood screws, screwing up through bottom of seat and into branch through the two inside holes on the 15" edge.

2. Attach the four predrilled branches to seat by screwing wood screws down through top of the seat and into branch; two screws have already been placed in Step 1.

3. Shape bark into a tube, overlapping 22" sides. Apply wood glue liberally to seams, and clamp in place until dry. Glue two 20" wood pieces along seams for support.

4. Measure the inside diameter of the tube and cut 20" pieces of wood to that measurement. Glue pieces inside tube, crisscrossing one another to brace tube. Secure braces to bark with wood screws. Glue sheet moss to top of seat, and top of plywood circle, overlapping 2" to bottom. Place moss-covered circle on top of bark tube.

**MOTHER NATURE'S GARDEN CAFE
SEAT DIAGRAM**

15"

2"
2"
3"

2"
2"

16"

Garden Butterfly

Materials

Ladder-back chair
Wooden butterfly cut from $1/2$"-thick wood (pattern provided)
24" length of $1/4$"-diameter dowel
Two clay pots
Black, blue, coral, gray, green, peach, purple, off-white, and
    yellow acrylic paints
Acrylic primer/sealer
Wood deck sealer
Elastic and reflective roof coating
Wood glue
Wood putty
Fine-grain sandpaper
Paintbrushes
Drill with $1/4$" bit
Saw
Photocopy machine

Instructions

1. Cut out middle bar from chair back; sand with sandpaper if needed. Putty holes and let dry. Paint chair with primer.

2. Using photocopy machine, enlarge butterfly pattern to fit into space where middle bar was removed. Transfer pattern to wood and cut out. Mark holes for dowel placement at top wing mark and lower wing mark. Drill holes through chair sides at each mark. Drill a hole at top and bottom marks on wings. Cut dowel into four equal pieces. Note: When assembled, four dowels will slip through side holes and into holes in butterfly's wings. Dowel length may need to be adjusted, depending upon how much space was between the chair back uprights.

3. Paint butterfly with acrylic primer. When dry, paint picture on butterfly, referring to adjacent butterfly paint pattern on page 40. Note: If desired, obtain a color photocopy of the pattern and découpage to butterfly. Pattern may need to be enlarged.

4. Paint chair legs and bars in different pastel colors. When dry, designs such as polka dots, diamonds, marbleizing, and wavy lines may be added. Paint seat off-white with a black diamond pattern.

5. Put wood glue into all drill holes, and insert dowels through holes in chair sides and into butterfly. Put wood putty into holes where dowels slid through, and paint to match chair.

6. Coat inside of pots with roof coating; paint outside of pots with acrylic primer. When dry, paint outside of pots to match designs on chair. Coat all surfaces with deck sealer.

BUTTERFLY PATTERN

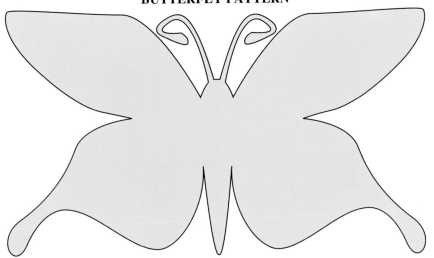

ENLARGE PATTERN TO FIT SPACE BETWEEN CHAIR BACK UPRIGHTS

Shades Of Battenburg Lace

Materials

Patio table with umbrella stand
Two rectangular Battenburg lace tablecloths
Four square Battenburg lace napkins

Instructions

1. Drape tablecloths across each other over the umbrella.

2. Place square napkins around tablecloths to fill any gaps.

BUTTERFLY PAINT PATTERN

INSTRUCTIONS FOR GARDEN BUTTERFLY ON PAGE 39

BIRDHOUSE POTTING TABLE DIAGRAMS

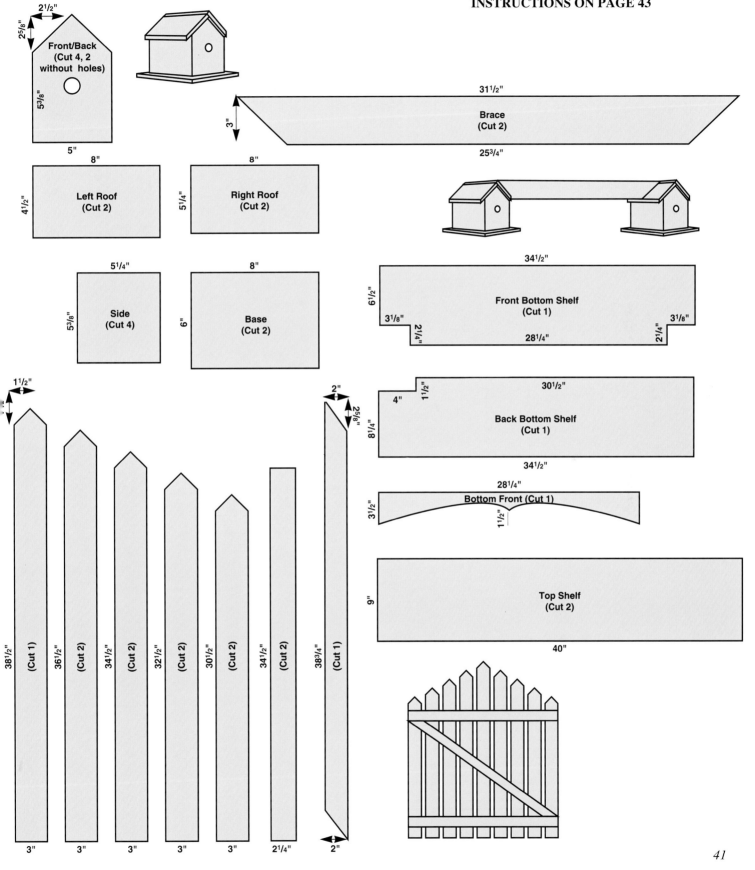

2¹/₂"

2⁵/₈"

Front/Back
(Cut 4, 2
without holes)

5³/₈"

5"

31¹/₂"

Brace
(Cut 2)

3"

25³/₄"

8"

Left Roof
(Cut 2)

4¹/₂"

8"

Right Roof
(Cut 2)

5¹/₄"

5¹/₄"

Side
(Cut 4)

5³/₈"

8"

Base
(Cut 2)

6"

34¹/₂"

Front Bottom Shelf
(Cut 1)

6¹/₂"

3¹/₈"   3¹/₈"

2¹/₄"   28¹/₄"   2¹/₄"

30¹/₂"

Back Bottom Shelf
(Cut 1)

1¹/₂"

4"

8¹/₄"

34¹/₂"

28¹/₄"

Bottom Front (Cut 1)

3¹/₂"

1¹/₂"

9"

Top Shelf
(Cut 2)

40"

1¹/₂"

2"

2⁵/₈"

38¹/₂"
(Cut 1)

36¹/₂"
(Cut 2)

34¹/₂"
(Cut 2)

32¹/₂"
(Cut 2)

30¹/₂"
(Cut 2)

34¹/₂"
(Cut 2)

38³/₄"
(Cut 1)

3"   3"   3"   3"   3"   2¹/₄"   2"

41

Plant Yourself At Rosie's Cafe

Materials

72" square piece of ³/4"-thick pine
Two banister posts (19" high, 10" diameter; blocks at base of posts measure 4¹/2" high, 3" wide)
Miniature rolling pin
Miniature garden shovel
Black, dark blue, light creamy gold, dark green, dark purple, dark rust, dark turquoise, and white acrylic paints
Wood primer
Wood deck sealer
Dark red floor-and-deck enamel
Wood glue
Paint thinner
Fine-grain sandpaper
Paintbrushes
Rags
Clamp
Hammer and nails
Drill with 1" hole saw bit
Table saw

Instructions

1. Cut all pieces according to patterns on page 41. Drill holes in two birdhouse fronts. Label all pieces.

2. Glue top shelf planks together, forming a 18" x 40" shelf. Clamp and let set one hour. Glue bottom shelf planks together to form a 17" x 34¹/2" shelf. Clamp and let set one hour.

3. Assemble back piece by placing pickets vertically, as in the diagram on page 41, about 1" apart on work surface. Use one brace as a guide to straighten bottom. Place top brace horizontally across pickets, 1¹/2" down from shortest post. Place other brace across pickets 2¹/2" up from bottom. Angled brace should fit diagonally between top and bottom braces. When everything is in place, nail together.

4. Assemble birdhouses as in the diagram, but do not attach roof. Center a birdhouse base on top of each banister post and nail in place. Center birdhouses onto bases and nail in place. Attach roofs to birdhouses.

5. Nail curved piece to underside of bottom shelf flush with front edge.

6. Stand picket back upright. Nail bottom shelf onto ridge along lower edge. Glue banisters (table legs) into place in cut-out portions of bottom shelf.

7. Nail top center piece between birdhouses 4¹/2" back from roof front.

8. Lay top shelf in place. Nail to ridge across back and along front center piece.

9. Sand table as needed and paint with wood primer.

10. Paint wood surfaces with wood primer.

11. Paint tabletop and lower shelf with dark red floor-and-deck enamel.

12. Paint pickets white.

13. Paint legs and birdhouses as desired, alternating colors.

14. Over one birdhouse hole, paint "Rosie's Cafe," and glue miniature rolling pin under hole as a perch. Over other birdhouse hole, paint "Violet's Herb Garden," and glue miniature garden shovel as a perch.

15. Sand entire table to distress.

16. Wipe with dark purple, dark blue, and black to add depth.

17. Paint all of table, except top and lower shelf, with deck sealer.

Breakfast For The Birds

Materials

Six 96" lengths of 2" x 8" redwood
144" length of 2" x 2" cedar
Fifteen 30" lengths of 2" x 4" cedar
Four 96" lengths of 1" x 6" redwood
130-150 zinc screws, 3" long
Black, dark blue, dark green, dark purple, and dark turquoise acrylic paints
Wood primer
Wood deck sealer
Dark red floor-and-deck enamel
Paint thinner
Paintbrushes
Wood glue
Circular saw
Drill with 2" hole saw bit
Fine-grain sandpaper
Rags

Instructions

1. For tabletop, place the six 96" redwood boards side by side. Measure the two center boards to 72" and cut. The boards connected to the middle boards will be cut at a 45-degree angle. The outside boards will be cut at a 45-degree angle to previous boards; see Diagram A on page 46.

2. Cut two 40" lengths of 2" x 2" cedar and place one strip perpendicular at 1-foot 6" from each end of underside of table top; see Diagram A on page 46. Attach with two zinc screws at each redwood board crossed.

3. Cut strips of 2" x 2" cedar to fit on ends and angles. Attach with two zinc screws at each redwood board crossed.

4. For center leg, cut three 2" x 4" cedar boards 30" long. Cut two 1" x 6" redwood boards 30" long. Place the three cedar boards together to form one block. On each side, place a redwood board. See Diagram B on page 46. Mark drill holes on redwood boards at each cedar board across top and bottom. Remove redwood boards and drill holes. Place redwood back on each side of cedar and screw in place.

5. Use the 2" hole saw to cut three holes on redwood sides of center leg. The holes should be spaced evenly and drilled 1" deep. See Diagram B on page 46.

6. From the extra 1" x 6" redwood, cut 12 pieces $1^1/4$" wide. Glue pieces together two at a time in an "L" shape to form platforms; see Diagram B on page 46. Glue each platform below a hole on the front and back of center leg; see Diagram B on page 46.

7. For the four exterior legs, follow same directions for center leg, except the holes and platforms will be on the outside only. The center cedar board may be left out to create an open space in leg; see Diagram C on page 46.

8. Cut eight 1"-wide pieces from 1" x 6" redwood. Miter one end of each strip to form a 45-degree angle; see Diagram C on page 46. Glue two strips together to form "roofs." Glue each roof in place at top of each exterior leg.

9. Connect tabletop and legs together by screwing zinc screws through the tabletop into legs. Exterior legs should rest against braces on underside of table. For extra leg strength, insert screws through braces into each leg.

10. Sand edges as needed. Paint all wood surfaces with wood primer.

11. Paint tabletop with dark red floor-and-deck enamel.

12. Paint legs dark turquoise, dark purple, and dark green. Paint birdhouse holes black.

13. Sand tabletop and legs to distress.

14. Wipe black and dark blue paint lightly over colors to add depth.

15. Paint all of table, except top, with deck sealer.

BREAKFAST FOR THE BIRDS DIAGRAMS

DIAGRAM A

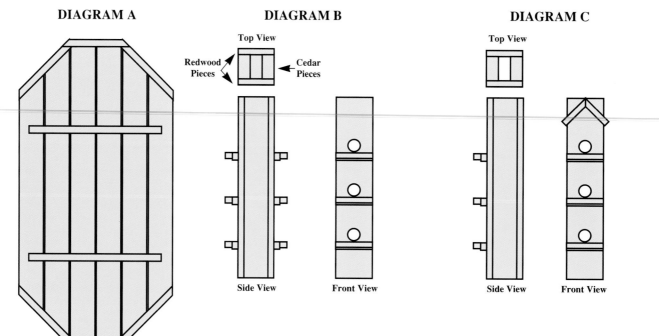

DIAGRAM B

Top View

Redwood Pieces → ← Cedar Pieces

Side View   Front View

DIAGRAM C

Top View

Side View   Front View

A FEAST FOR THE EYES BENCH PATTERN

A FEAST FOR THE EYES INSTRUCTIONS ON PAGE 48

A Feast For The Eyes

A Feast For The Eyes

Materials

Picnic table (or any outdoor table)
Four packages of cocktail-size printed paper napkins (model has green-leafed background with grapes)
Forest-green and three shades of purple acrylic paints
Large bottle of découpage glue
Wood primer
Satin finish varnish
Paint thinner
Paintbrushes

Instructions

1. Paint table with wood primer and let dry. Paint tabletop, benches, and assorted legs forest-green. Paint other legs with three shades of purple.

2. Separate top layer from napkins and discard second layer. Découpage napkins onto tabletop and edge.

3. Paint benches, following pattern on the background of the napkins or use model pattern on page 46. Note: Benches may also be découpaged, depending on use. (Rough pant pockets or children rough-housing may scratch a découpaged surface.)

4. Varnish table and benches with satin varnish, following manufacturer's instructions.

It is recommended that découpaged objects be brought indoors during inclement weather. Rain may cause découpaged surface to turn white, but it should return to its original color when dry.

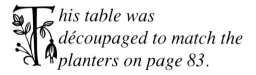

This table was découpaged to match the planters on page 83.

Fabric-Wrapped Patio Chair

Materials

Metal patio chair
Seat for chair cut from $3/4$"-thick plywood
Large pot to fit in chair seat
1 yard each of two coordinating cotton fabrics
Acrylic paints for detail
Assorted jewels to embellish
Large bottle of découpage glue
Acrylic primer/sealer
Elastic and reflective roof coating
Paintbrushes
Saw

Instructions

1. Paint inside of pot with roof coating and let dry. Paint outside of pot with acrylic primer and let dry.

2. Cut a hole in chair seat big enough to place pot. Pot should sit halfway down into seat.

3. Tear fabric into 1"-wide strips. Beginning at bottom of chair leg, brush a small section of chair leg with découpage glue and wrap fabric around. Overlap fabric so that metal does not show through. Continue until chair is completely covered, alternating fabrics as desired.

4. Cover outside of pot and chair seat in same manner.

5. Apply two more coats of découpage glue to all surfaces.

6. If chair has a place where painting or jewels can be added, embellish as desired.

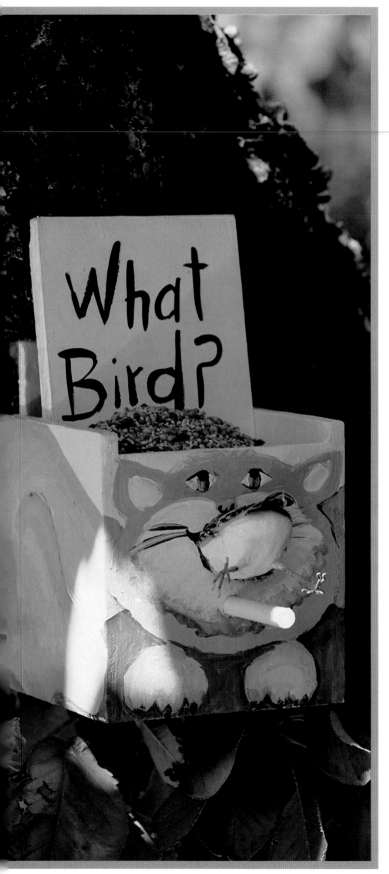

Who Me? What Bird?

Materials

30" x 7" piece of $^3/_8$"-thick plywood
3" length of $^3/_8$"-diameter wooden dowel
One artificial stuffed bird
Black, light blue, light gray, gray, dark gray, pink, and white acrylic paints
Wood primer
Wood deck sealer
Wood glue
Paintbrushes
Hammer and finishing nails
Drill with $^1/_8$" and $^3/_8$" bits and 1" hole saw bit
Photocopy machine

Instructions

1. Cut wood according to diagram on opposite page. With $^3/_8$" bit, drill a hole in the center $^1/_2$" from top of back piece. Drill a hole in center of front piece 3" down from top. With 1" hole saw bit, drill a hole about $^1/_2$" above other hole in front piece; see diagram. With $^1/_8$" bit, drill holes in the $5^1/_4$" sides of the lid 1" down from the top edge.

2. Nail front and back pieces between side pieces. Drop bottom piece inside and nail in place.

3. Mark on each side $1^1/_2$" from back and $^1/_8$" down from top edge. Place lid on top of birdhouse with drill holes toward back. Hammer a nail at each mark through to lid. Note: Nails should go into drill holes on sides of lid and serve as hinges.

4. Paint birdhouse with wood primer. When dry, paint with a base coat of white; let dry. Using photocopy machine, enlarge cat patterns on opposite page 200%. Transfer patterns to box and paint. Lift lid and paint "What Bird?" in black. Coat entire birdhouse with deck sealer. Glue dowel into hole in front, and glue bird into mouth.

CAT PATTERNS

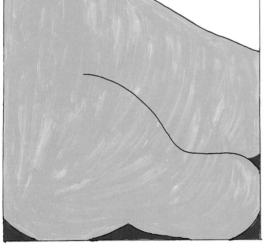

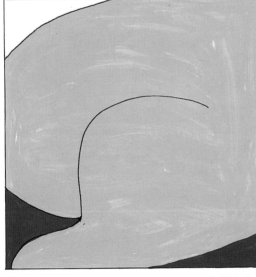

ENLARGE PATTERNS 200%

BIRDHOUSE DIAGRAM

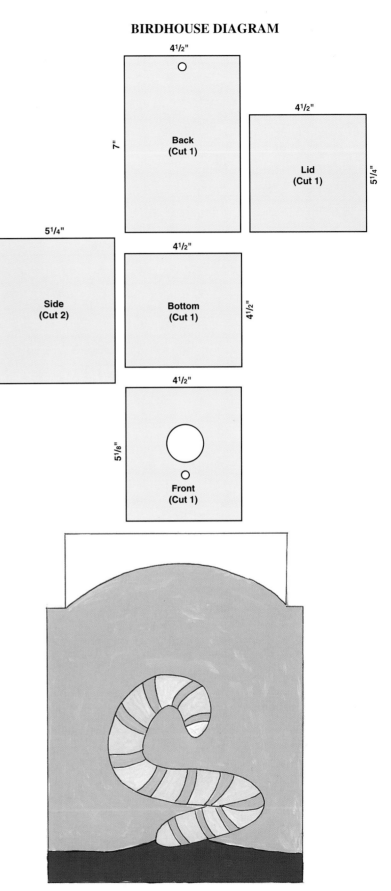

4¹/₂"

○

7"

**Back
(Cut 1)**

4¹/₂"

**Lid
(Cut 1)**

5¹/₄"

5¹/₄"

5¹/₂"

**Side
(Cut 2)**

4¹/₂"

**Bottom
(Cut 1)**

4¹/₂"

4¹/₂"

5¹/₈"

○

**Front
(Cut 1)**

Hummingbird Patio Gazebo

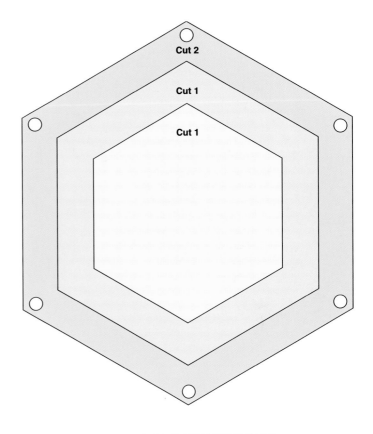

Cut 2

Cut 1

Cut 1

ENLARGE PATTERNS 200%

Materials

48-ounce hexagon hummingbird feeder
1" x 8" x 48" piece of pine board
Six 9" turned dowels
$4^1/_2$" wood finial
Brass eye hook
Six 1" kotter keys
Greenery vine
Small roses
One package of floral-print cocktail napkins
White acrylic paint
Wood primer
Wood deck sealer
Découpage glue
Wood glue
Industrial-strength glue
Paintbrushes
Drill with $^3/_8$" and $^1/_{16}$" bits
Band or table saw
Router
Photocopy machine

Instructions

1. Using photocopy machine, enlarge hexagon patterns 200%. Transfer patterns to pine board and cut out. Using the router, cut around all sides of three of the shapes, leaving one large hexagon flat.

2. With wood glue, glue the three routed shapes on top of each other, from largest to smallest.

3. Drill holes about $^1/_4$" deep in underside of largest routed shape, following markings in pattern. Drill holes completely through large flat shape, following markings in pattern.

4. Brush all wood pieces with wood primer and let dry.

5. Paint all wood pieces, except finial, with two coats of white paint. Let dry. Coat with deck sealer.

6. Glue dowels into the gazebo top holes with wood glue.

7. If necessary, pop out small feeding flowers from bottom of feeder. Découpage bottom of feeder and finial with floral napkins. Leave feeding holes open.

8. Place feeder on base. Place gazebo top over feeder, sliding dowels into holes in base. Drill very small holes through sides of dowels about $^1/_8$" up from bottom. Insert kotter keys. The keys hold the base in place and are pulled to remove feeder.

9. Screw brass eye hook into top of finial, and glue to top of gazebo. Cascade and glue greenery around top and down side of gazebo. Glue roses to greenery.

Room With A View

Materials

Large wooden frame (model is 29" x 17" x 1")
10" x 20" piece of $^3/_4$"-thick wood
$1^1/_2$"-diameter wooden handrail or closet rod, 5' long
Birdhouse to fit in center of frame
$^1/_4$"-diameter screw, 5" long
Cup hook
Gray and off-white acrylic paints
Wood primer
Wood deck sealer
Wood glue
Fine-grain sandpaper
Paintbrushes
Paper towel
Awl
Scroll saw
Clamps
Drill with $^1/_4$" bit

Instructions

1. Enlarge patterns on opposite page. Transfer patterns to $^3/_4$"-wide wood and cut out. Sand edges smooth.

2. Paint all wood pieces with wood primer. When dry, paint all pieces off-white.

3. Thin gray paint with a little water and wash over off-white paint, wiping off any excess paint with a paper towel.

4. With wood glue and clamps, attach scroll pieces to top and inside corners of frame. Let set.

5. With an awl, make a hole on the underside center top of the frame. Screw in the cup hook and paint gray.

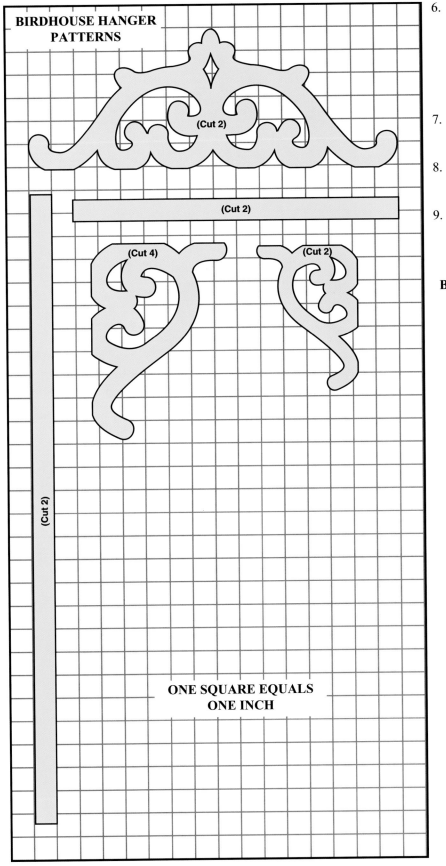

BIRDHOUSE HANGER PATTERNS

(Cut 2)

(Cut 2)

(Cut 4)

(Cut 2)

(Cut 2)

**ONE SQUARE EQUALS
ONE INCH**

6. Drill a hole in the bottom center of frame. Drill a hole in one end of the handrail. Place wood glue in the drilled hole in handrail. Insert the screw through the hole in the frame, and secure into the hole in handrail. Paint head of screw gray.

7. Glue remaining two pieces of scrollwork to each side of handrail at base of frame.

8. Apply deck sealer, following manufacturer's instructions.

9. Hang birdhouse from hook.

BIRDHOUSE HANGER DIAGRAM

55

The Cow Over The Moon

Materials

48"-square piece of $3/4$"-thick wood (use old wood for a
 weathered look)
10" x 12" piece of $1/4$"-thick plywood
6" length of $5/16$"-diameter wooden dowel
2 yards of heavy black wire
Black, white, yellow, violet-blue, and slate-gray acrylic paints
Wood primer
Wood deck sealer
Wood glue
Paintbrushes
Hammer and nails
Pliers
Wire cutters
Drill with $3/16$" and $5/16$" bits and 2" hole saw bit
Saw
Photocopy machine

Instructions

1. Cut wood according to diagram on page 58. Miter one
   long edge on each large roof piece so that, when joined,
   roof forms a peak flush with birdhouse points. Repeat for
   small roof, except miter one short edge of each piece.
   Notch other short edges as in diagram. Drill 2" holes and
   $5/16$" holes in front piece, as in diagram.

2. Nail large step to bottom of front piece and small step on
   top of large step. Construct birdhouse by placing side
   pieces between front and back pieces and nailing into
   place. Nail large roof pieces together, and attach to top of
   house. Nail small roof pieces together, and glue above
   bottom hole. Cut dowel in half, and glue each piece into
   $5/16$" holes in front of house.

3. Using photocopy machine, enlarge moon, star, and cow
   patterns on page 58 to 200%. Transfer patterns to
   plywood and cut out. Paint all wood with wood primer
   and let dry. Paint birdhouse violet-blue, roof slate-gray,
   stars and moon yellow, and cow white and black.

4. Drill four holes with $3/16$" bit randomly in roof. Drill hole
   in bottom of cow, stars, and moon.

5. Cut wire into five equal lengths. Glue one wire into each
   shape. Use pliers to bend and curl wire. Glue shapes into
   holes in roof.

6. Coat entire project with deck sealer.

Rabbit Transit, Garden Style

Materials

One 4-cubic-foot red wheelbarrow
One 66" x 40" piece of $1/2$"-thick wood
Two wood blocks 1" x $1^1/2$" x 18"
Six wood screws
Black, light blue, blue, light brown, brown, dark brown,
 light pink, red, and white acrylic paints
Wood primer
Wood deck sealer
Fine-grain sandpaper
Paintbrushes
Hammer and nails
Drill

Instructions

1. Enlarge rabbit pattern on page 58. Transfer pattern to
   wood and cut out two rabbits; sand with sandpaper if
   needed. Paint wood with primer and let dry.

3. Paint rabbit onto both sides of each cutout, following
   pattern. When dry, paint with deck sealer.

4. Attach wood blocks horizontally at each side of wheelbarrow by drilling three holes through blocks and wheelbarrow and inserting screws at sides and center of block.

5. Mount rabbit to wheelbarrow. Secure to blocks with nails.

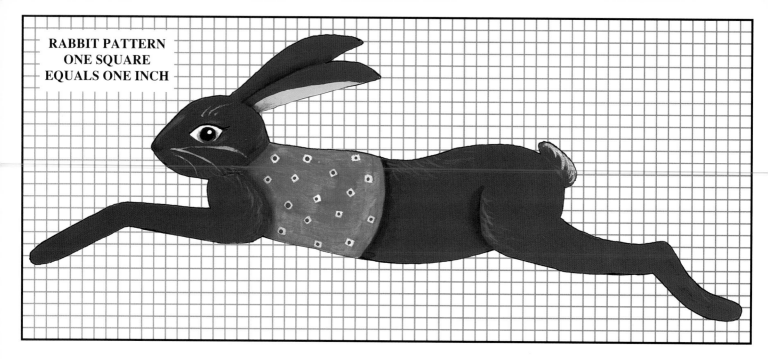

**RABBIT PATTERN
ONE SQUARE
EQUALS ONE INCH**

THE COW OVER THE MOON DIAGRAMS

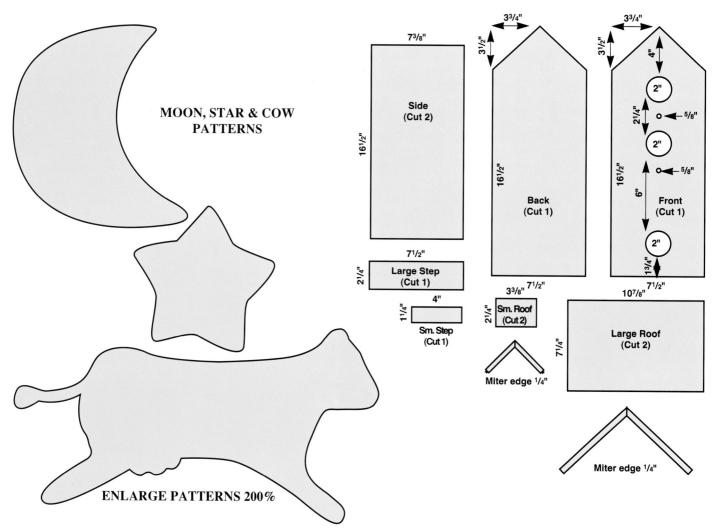

**MOON, STAR & COW
PATTERNS**

ENLARGE PATTERNS 200%

7³/₈"

Side
(Cut 2)

16¹/₂"

3³/₄"

3¹/₂"

Back
(Cut 1)

16¹/₂"

3³/₄"

3¹/₂"

4"

2"

2¹/₄"

5/₈"

2"

5/₈"

16¹/₂"

6"

Front
(Cut 1)

2"

1³/₄"

7¹/₂"

Large Step
(Cut 1)

2¹/₄"

1¹/₄"

4"

Sm. Step
(Cut 1)

3³/₈"   7¹/₂"

2¹/₄"   Sm. Roof
(Cut 2)

Miter edge ¹/₄"

7¹/₂"

10⁷/₈"

7¹/₄"

Large Roof
(Cut 2)

Miter edge ¹/₄"

Rabbit Transit, Garden Style

Illumination

Give A Little Garden Light

Materials
23" x 15" piece of chicken wire
3^1/$_4$"-diameter brass ring
24" of 16-gauge silver wire
Decorative copper wire
Pliers
Wire cutters
Work gloves

Instructions
It is recommended that a work shirt or apron be worn when working with chicken wire used in this project.

1. Bring short sides of chicken wire together, forming a tube. Thread silver wire down seam to secure.

2. Cinch one end of chicken wire tube to fit around brass ring. Place brass ring inside, and wrap ends of chicken wire around ring with pliers. (Make certain the rows of chicken wire are even all around.)

3. Twist the opposite end of tube tightly together. Pull out sides and shape into a sphere.

4. Wrap top of candle guard with decorative copper wire.

By The Sea, By The Sea

Materials
Two tall wooden candlesticks
One wooden bowl
Assorted seashells
Chartreuse, fuchsia, metallic gold, purple, and bright yellow acrylic paints
Wood deck sealer
Paintbrushes
Hot glue gun and glue sticks

Instructions
1. Paint candlesticks and bowl as desired with all colors, except metallic gold.

2. Paint shells as desired, and highlight with metallic gold.

3. Hot-glue shells onto candlesticks, and place remaining shells in bowl. Coat entire project with deck sealer.

Paper~Cup Lawn Torches

Materials for Six

Six paper party cups in desired designs
Six wooden candle cups with $5/8$" opening
Six $5/8$"-diameter wooden dowels in desired length
Six small votive cups
Six votive candles
Acrylic paints in desired colors
Craft knife
Hot glue gun and glue sticks
Paintbrushes

Instructions

1. Make sure candle cups fit over ends of dowels. Paint dowels and candle cups to match party cups.

2. With craft knife, cut designs from party cups, partially cutting some designs. Bend partial cut designs outward, and completely remove fully cut portions. Note: For easier cutting, begin in center of design and work toward outer edges of pattern. This will help center to stay intact and keep the cup stable while cutting.

3. Hot-glue bottom of votive cups to inside bottom of party cups. Place on top of dowels.

4. Place candles in votive cups inside party cups. Note: This lawn torch should be used for special occasions only, since paper cup will not hold up well against elements.

Try using different types and styles of paper cups for various seasons or party themes.

Flower-Petal Lawn Torch

Materials

Ten 3" artificial magnolia flower petals
Three 6" artificial leaves
4" cardboard cone (model made with thread cone)
Votive cup and candle
48" length of $5/8$"-diameter dowel
Floral tape
2 yards of 1"-diameter dark green braid or rope
Brown and metallic gold acrylic paints
Matte spray sealer
Paintbrushes
Hot glue gun and glue sticks

Instructions

1. Push dowel into small end of cone about 2" and hot-glue.

2. Hot-glue petals around outer top edge of cone, overlapping as necessary.

3. Starting at top of cone, wrap floral tape around cone and 1" of dowel.

4. Paint dowel and wrapped cone brown.

5. Hot-glue leaves down dowel. Wrap braid around dowel and hot-glue.

6. Using dry-brush technique, highlight cone and dowel with metallic gold paint.

7. Spray entire lantern with matte sealer. Insert votive cup and candle in center. Note: This lantern should be used for special occasions only, since flower petals will not hold up well against elements.

Lantern To Light Up The Season

Materials
One 4$\frac{1}{2}$"-tall cup-shaped drinking glass
Votive candle
Sand
3$\frac{1}{2}$ yards of tie wire
Natural colored twine
Large-eyed needle
Pliers
Wire cutters

Instructions
1. Cut three 40" lengths of tie wire. Bundle the lengths of wire together, and tie a length of twine around center to secure. Using needle, slip ends of twine through knot and cut off excess.

2. Place glass at center of wires on knot. Wrap wires around sides of glass, and secure in place with a temporary length of twine. Space wires equal distance from one another around sides of glass.

3. Begin $\frac{1}{4}$" from top of glass with needle threaded with twine, and knot twine around one wire. Wrap and loop stitch around each wire until top $\frac{1}{4}$" of the glass is covered.

4. Secure wire and twine intersections with a cross-stitch. Tie twine off at end and hide ends under wrapping.

5. Remove temporary length of twine around top of glass.

6. Separate free ends of wire into two groups of three wires each. Bend each group into a half circle. Join half circles together at top, forming a handle. Using pliers, twist wires together to secure.

7. Fill glass with sand and place votive candle inside.

Lantern Hook

Materials
One $\frac{1}{2}$" cup hook
48" length of $\frac{3}{4}$"-diameter wooden dowel
$\frac{3}{4}$"-diameter PVC conduit L-joint
10 yards of size #72 four-ply jute
Hot glue gun and glue sticks
Small handsaw

Instructions
1. Using handsaw, cut a 3" length from the wooden dowel; set remaining length aside. Insert into one end of PVC L-joint. Screw cup hook onto end of dowel.

2. Push remaining piece of dowel into other end of PVC L-joint.

3. Beginning at cup hook end, wrap jute around dowel and PVC L-joint, stopping 9" from end of dowel. Secure ends of jute with hot glue.

4. Hang lantern from hook.

Wrap dowels with 1" strips of fabric, colored twine, or ribbons to match a party's theme or decorations.

Midsummer's Night Light

Materials

Small glass vase (wide enough to accommodate a votive candle)
Small ivy garland
20" of heavy wire
Votive candle
Florist tape
Dirt
Pliers
Wire cutters

Instructions

1. Cut a length of wire to fit around neck of vase. Cover with florist tape and attach to vase by twisting ends together. Cut a length of wire for handle and cover with florist tape. Attach to each side of vase by twisting through neck wire.

2. Twist ivy around neck and handle, and secure with florist tape if needed.

3. Fill vase with about an inch of dirt. Set candle into dirt.

4. Hang vase from lantern hook.

Fill vase with small wooden beads, tiny rocks, marbles, or colored sand for different lantern variations.

Laguna Beach Party Lantern

Materials
One 7"-tall vase with neck
Votive candle
Nine seashells
Sand
2 yards of tie wire
Craft glue
Pliers
Wire cutters

Instructions

1. Find the center point of the 2-yard length of tie wire. Hold this point firmly against the neck of the vase. Wrap one end of the wire around vase and back to the center. Twist wires together to secure. Wrap remaining lengths of the wires in opposite directions until you have a 12" tail. Loop tail through wrapped wire to secure. Using pliers, bring both ends up to the top and twist ends together tightly to form handle. Clip off excess wire.

2. Glue shells around bottom of vase, alternating the direction of the shells.

3. Fill bottom of vase 2" deep with sand.

4. Place votive candle inside vase in sand.

"It's A Wrap" Patio Lights

Materials

One string of small outdoor/indoor Christmas lights
One $4^1/2$" square of thin wrapping paper for each light
Glue
Scissors
Pinking shears (optional)

Instructions

1. Fold wrapping-paper square from corner to corner. Cut $^1/_2$" off top corner.

2. Open square and fold corners to center. Overlap flaps to fold lines and glue in place, forming lamp shade; be certain top opening is large enough for light to slip into. Trim edges with pinking shears if desired. Slip lamp shade over light.

3. Repeat to cover remaining lights. Note: These lights should be used for special occasions only, since wrapping paper will not hold up well against elements.

DIAGRAM

Bird's & Bee's Patio Lights

Floral Bird Cage Variation Materials

One string of small outdoor/indoor Christmas lights
Small wire bird cages (one for each light)
An assortment of very small dried or silk flowers and leaves
Florist's clay
Hot glue gun and glue sticks

Instructions

1. If necessary, cut away a portion of wire at top front and back of bird cages to string lights through.

2. Starting at top of cage, press florist's clay down one side and around bottom. Hot-glue flowers and leaves to clay.

3. Thread lights through bird cages.

Beehive Variation Materials

One string of small outdoor/indoor Christmas lights
Small wire bird cages (one for each light)
Artificial bees (two or three per cage)
1/4"-diameter twine
Hot glue gun and glue sticks

Instructions

Photo on page 60.

1. Follow Step 1 of Floral Bird Cage Variation above.

2. Wrap and hot-glue twine around cage to resemble a beehive.

3. Hot-glue bees to beehive as desired.

4. Thread lights through beehive.

Garland Of Petal Delight

Materials
One strand of small red outdoor/indoor Christmas lights
Ivory silk roses (one for each light)
Green silk leaf sprigs (a silk plant works well)
Hot glue gun and glue sticks

Instructions
1. Separate rose petals. Insert a light through the center of petals. Rebuild the rose around a light as the flower center.

2. Hot-glue leaves on both sides of each light.

Paper-Cup Patio Lights

Materials
One string of small outdoor/indoor Christmas lights
White or solid-colored paper cups (one for each light)
Large pin
Craft knife

Instructions
1. Lightly transfer pattern onto cup.

2. Using a craft knife, cut solid lines on pattern. Slightly push petals and leaves inward to allow light to pass through. Using a pin, poke design above and below pattern.

3. Cut a small hole at the center bottom of cup for light.

4. Unscrew Christmas light and push it up through hole in top of cup. Screw light back into the socket.

5. Repeat with remaining lights. Note: This lantern should be used for special occasions only, since flower petals will not hold up well against elements.

FLOWER PATTERN

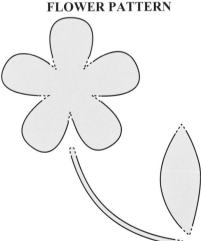

Cultivation

Plant "Tree Of A Kind"

Materials

46" x 29" piece of $1/2$"-thick redwood
85 to 100 small finishing nails
Redwood stain
Wood deck sealer
Paintbrushes
Fine-grain sandpaper
Hammer
Saw

Instructions

1. Cut five $1/2$" x 1" x 25" and three $1/2$" x 1" x 9" pieces of redwood for bottom. Cut two sides from redwood; see Diagram A. Cut ten $1/2$" x $1 3/4$" x 29" pieces of redwood for front and back.

2. Place five $1/2$" x 1" x 25" slats on their sides. Miter ends by cutting away portion indicated by the dotted line in Diagram B. Place slats horizontally on work surface 1" apart with mitered short edge facing up. Place three $1/2$" x 1" x 9" slats vertically at sides and center for braces; see Diagram C. Make certain side braces are flush with short edge. Nail in place.

3. Nail side boards to bottom sides $2 1/4$" up from bottom; see Diagram D.

4. Cut boards for front and back according to Diagram E. Nail front slats in five rows between side boards, starting flush at top with longest board and continuing down to bottom edge; see Diagram E. Place boards $5/16$" apart.

5. Sand all boards as needed. Stain with redwood stain. When completely dry, brush with deck sealer, following manufacturer's instructions.

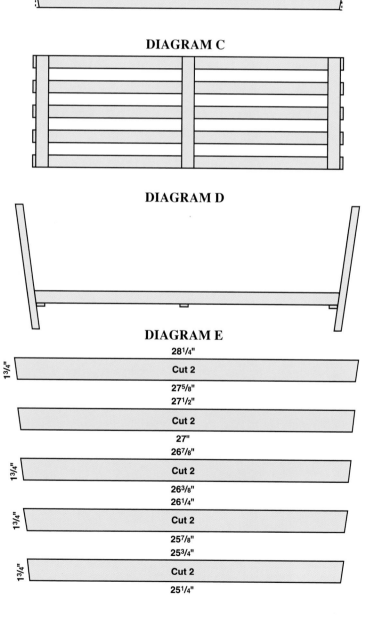

DIAGRAM A

9"
Side
Cut 2
$10 1/8$"
$5 1/2$"
2"
$1 1/4$"
$1 1/4$"

DIAGRAM B

DIAGRAM C

DIAGRAM D

DIAGRAM E

$28 1/4$"
$1 3/4$"
Cut 2
$27 5/8$"
$27 1/2$"
Cut 2
27"
$26 7/8$"
$1 3/4$"
Cut 2
$26 3/8$"
$26 1/4$"
$1 3/4$"
Cut 2
$25 7/8$"
$25 3/4$"
$1 3/4$"
Cut 2
$25 1/4$"

Plant Sitter Critters

Materials

Three 14" squares of $3/4$"-thick plywood
Three 18" lengths of $3/8$" wooden dowels
Blue, light blue, black, brown, burgundy, gray, light gray, green, mauve, light mauve, orange, peach, light peach, pink, tan, white, and pale yellow acrylic paints
Matte spray sealer
Acrylic primer/sealer
Fine-grain sandpaper
Graphite paper
Tracing paper
Brown paper sack
Permanent fine-tip black marker
Paintbrushes
Drill with $3/8$" bit
Saw
Photocopy machine

Instructions

1. Using photocopy machine, enlarge critter patterns on page 78 to 275%. Trace patterns onto tracing paper. Place graphite paper on wood and lay patterns on top. Trace patterns onto wood. Cut shapes and sand edges.

2. Drill a hole in the bottom of each cutout to insert dowel.

3. Paint all pieces with acrylic primer. Crumple brown paper sack and rub over surface to be painted. This makes the surface smoother for painting. Paint each cutout according to color chart and pattern, first painting a base coat of each color, then adding shading as indicated. Let dry.

4. Draw detail with fine-tip marker. Spray with a light coat of matte sealer to keep the marker from smearing; let dry.

5. When completely dry, insert dowels.

COLOR CHART

BUNNY
Body tan with brown shading
Eyes white, black, and brown
Basket pale yellow
Carrots orange
Carrot tops green
Coat medium blue with blue shading
Ears and nose light peach

SKUNK
Body black with white stripe
Eye white, black, and brown
Dress burgundy with light mauve shading
Pinafore mauve with light mauve shading

MOUSE
Body gray with light gray shading
Eyes white, green, and black
Nose and ears pink
Dress rust with cream shading
Apron peach with cream shading

Plant sitters can be made to accentuate a patio or party theme. Use figures from storybooks, coloring books, or wrapping paper.

ENLARGE PATTERNS 275%

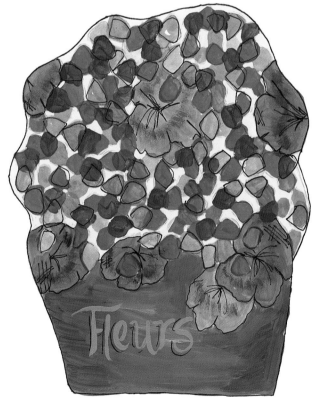

ENLARGE PATTERNS 200%

Please Don't Fence Me In

Materials

24" x 30" piece of 1/2"-thick wood
24" x 4" piece of 1/4"-thick wood
24" x 21" piece of chicken wire
Black, blue, brown, cream, green, dark green, light green, orange, pink, purple, light purple, red, white, and yellow acrylic paints
Acrylic primer/sealer
Wood deck sealer
Multipurpose cement glue
Fine-tip permanent black marker
Paintbrushes
Wire cutters
Hammer and nails
Staple gun
Saw
Photocopy machine

Instructions

1. From 1/2"-thick wood, cut four 8 1/2" x 1" pieces, four 10 1/2" x 1" pieces, and four 24" x 1" pieces. Also, cut two 9" x 1" pieces for base ends and eleven 9" x 1 1/2" pieces for base slats.

2. From 1/4"-thick wood, cut four 8 1/2" x 1/2" pieces, four 10 1/2" x 1/2" pieces, and four 24" x 1/2" pieces.

3. For ends, nail two 8 1/2" x 1" boards between two 10 1/2" x 1" boards, as in Diagram A. Repeat for other end. Cut two 10 1/2" squares of chicken wire, and staple one to each frame. Nail a 8 1/2" x 1/2" slat across the top and bottom along edge of chicken wire. Nail a 10 1/2" x 1/2" slat down sides along edges of chicken wire.

4. For front, place two 24" x 1" boards horizontally on work surface 8 1/2" apart. Cut a 24" x 10 1/2" piece of chicken wire and staple onto boards. Nail a 24" x 1/2" slat across the top and bottom, covering chicken-wire edge; see Diagram B. Repeat for back of planter.

5. With the chicken wire on the inside, nail the front and back pieces between the side pieces, forming a box.

6. Place 9" base pieces about 1/2" apart across bottom, starting with a 1" base end, followed by eleven 1 1/2" base slats and ending with a 1" base end. When all are even, nail in place.

7. Using a photocopy machine, enlarge flowerpot and butterfly patterns on page 79 to 200%. Transfer patterns to wood and cut out. Paint wooden flowerpots with acrylic primer. When dry, paint with acrylic paints following patterns.

8. Paint planter box with acrylic primer. When dry, paint light blue.

9. Glue painted flowerpot shapes to front of planter. Coat all wood with deck sealer.

DIAGRAM A **DIAGRAM B**

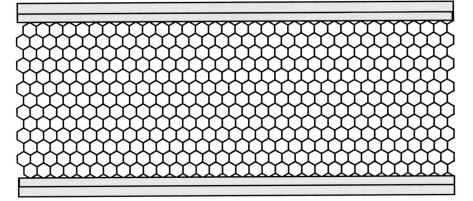

"Let It Pour"

Planter Materials

Four 30" rain-gutter sections
Eight rain-gutter end caps
Black, blue, green, purple, pink, and white acrylic paints
Acrylic primer/sealer
Matte spray varnish
Paintbrushes
Drill with $1/4$" bit
Photocopy machine

RAIN-GUTTER PATTERN

Instructions

1. Attach end caps to each rain-gutter section. Paint outside of rain-gutter section with acrylic primer. Let dry.

2. Paint all pieces with a blue base coat and allow to dry. Using photocopy machine, enlarge pattern to fit rain gutter. Transfer pattern onto rain gutters, and paint as shown, repeating pattern as necessary.

3. Drill several holes in the bottom of each rain gutter for drainage. Let dry, then coat with matte spray varnish.

Planter Mounting Materials

16 wood screw anchors #8 x 1"
16 screws #8 x 1"
Eight $3/4$"-long bolts with nuts
Eight 4" corner iron brackets
Drill with $1/4$" masonry bit and Phillips screwdriver bit
Hammer

Instructions

1. Mark position of corner brackets on brick. With masonry bit, drill holes marked. With hammer, tap in screw anchors. Position brackets and mount with screws. Repeat for all brackets.

2. Place rain-gutter planters onto brackets. Mark holes in bottom of rain gutter to match holes in bracket. Drill holes and bolt to bracket.

ENLARGE TO FIT RAIN GUTTER

Humpty Dumpty Laid The Egg

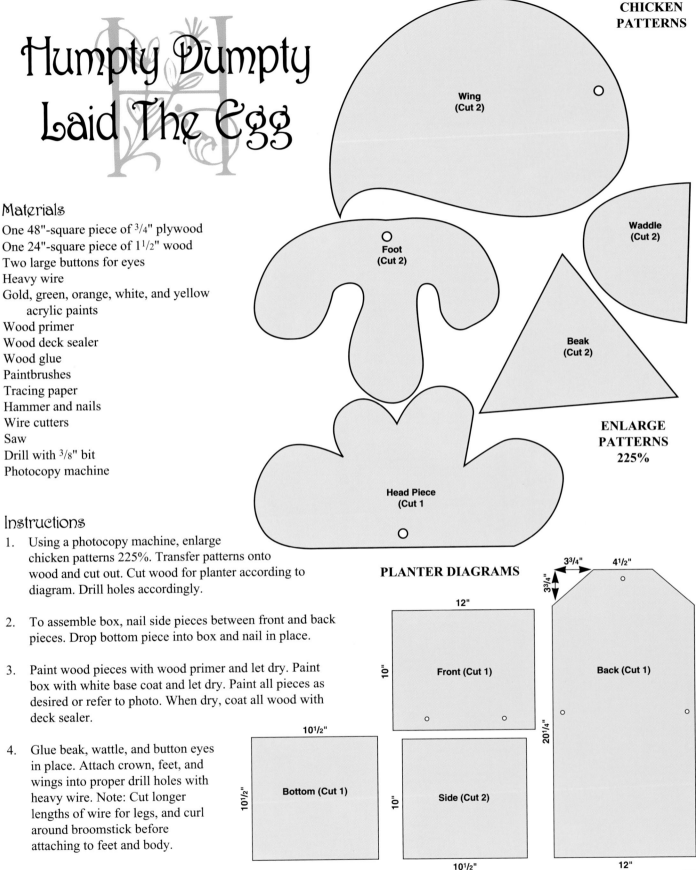

Materials

One 48"-square piece of ³/₄" plywood
One 24"-square piece of 1¹/₂" wood
Two large buttons for eyes
Heavy wire
Gold, green, orange, white, and yellow
    acrylic paints
Wood primer
Wood deck sealer
Wood glue
Paintbrushes
Tracing paper
Hammer and nails
Wire cutters
Saw
Drill with ³/₈" bit
Photocopy machine

Wing (Cut 2)

Waddle (Cut 2)

Foot (Cut 2)

Beak (Cut 2)

ENLARGE PATTERNS 225%

Head Piece (Cut 1

Instructions

1. Using a photocopy machine, enlarge chicken patterns 225%. Transfer patterns onto wood and cut out. Cut wood for planter according to diagram. Drill holes accordingly.

2. To assemble box, nail side pieces between front and back pieces. Drop bottom piece into box and nail in place.

3. Paint wood pieces with wood primer and let dry. Paint box with white base coat and let dry. Paint all pieces as desired or refer to photo. When dry, coat all wood with deck sealer.

4. Glue beak, wattle, and button eyes in place. Attach crown, feet, and wings into proper drill holes with heavy wire. Note: Cut longer lengths of wire for legs, and curl around broomstick before attaching to feet and body.

PLANTER DIAGRAMS

12"

10" **Front (Cut 1)**

3³/₄" 4¹/₂"

3³/₄"

20¹/₄" **Back (Cut 1)**

10¹/₂"

10¹/₂" **Bottom (Cut 1)**

10" **Side (Cut 2)**

10¹/₂"

12"

Mocha Tile Planter Box

Homemade-Tile Planter Box

Ceiling-Tile Planter Box

Cactus Rose Planter Box

Mocha Tile Planter Box

Homemade-Tile Planter Box

Materials

48"-square piece of $3/4$"-thick plywood
Eight $3^1/2$"-square tiles
Nails
Bits of string, yarn, and mesh ribbon
Berry, dark brown, and golden-tan acrylic paints
Wood glue
Découpage glue
Wood primer
Wood deck sealer
Paintbrushes
Fine-grain sandpaper
Hammer
Saw
Drill with $1/4$" bit

Instructions

1. From plywood, cut two 12" x 9" pieces for sides, two $17^1/2$" x 9" pieces for front and back, and one $15^1/2$" x 12" piece for bottom.

2. Construct box by nailing side pieces between front and back pieces. Drop bottom down inside box and nail in place. Sand as needed. Drill a few drainage holes in bottom of box.

3. Paint box with wood primer; let dry. Paint box golden-tan; let dry. Attach tiles as desired with wood glue.

4. Use découpage glue to attach string, yarn, and mesh ribbon as desired; let dry. Paint over raised textures with golden-tan, and blend swirls of dark brown and berry over box. When completely dry, coat with deck sealer.

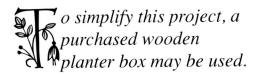

To simplify this project, a purchased wooden planter box may be used.

Materials

Five 5" squares of Plexiglas
Sculpting clay
Plaster of Paris
Cookie cutter in desired shapes
Assorted colors of acrylic paints
Wood primer
Wood deck sealer
Paintbrushes
Knife
Rolling pin
Fine-grain sandpaper
Wood glue
Wide tape

Instructions

1. Tape four pieces of Plexiglas together to form a box with no top or bottom.

2. Knead clay until soft and roll out to $1/4$" thickness. Use fifth piece of glass as a pattern to cut square from clay. Cut shape out of the center with a cookie cutter.

3. Place Plexiglas box over clay square. Mix plaster, following manufacturer's directions, and pour quickly into box about $1/4$" deep. Let set until dry. Note: To make multiple tiles, make additional Plexiglas boxes, as the drying time for the plaster is quite lengthy.

4. Push plaster mold out of bottom and remove clay. Let plaster dry completely. Sand edges until smooth.

5. Paint as desired; let dry. Make the Mocha Tile Planter Box, or purchase a rectangle planter box. Paint box with wood primer; let dry. Paint box as desired. When dry, attach tiles with glue. Coat with deck sealer.

Ceiling-Tile Planter Box

Materials

24" x 72" piece of $^3/4$"-thick wood
Two 1" x 1" x 96" strips of wood moulding
Four 23$^1/2$" x 12$^1/2$" pieces of tin ceiling sheeting
Gray, dark gray, and silver acrylic paints
Acrylic primer/sealer
Matte varnish
Paintbrushes
Tin shears
Hammer and nails
Drill with $^1/4$" bit
Saw

Instructions

1. From wood, cut two 24" x 11$^5/8$" pieces for front and back, two 11$^1/4$" x 11$^5/8$" pieces for sides, and one 22$^1/2$" x 11$^1/4$" piece for bottom.

2. Nail sides between front and back pieces of box. Drop bottom down inside box and nail in place. Sand as needed. Drill a few drainage holes in bottom of box. Coat with acrylic primer; let dry.

3. Nail tin onto the sides of the box, bringing tin over top and bottom edge. Cut eight pieces of moulding, each 11$^5/8$" long. Nail one piece at a corner edge, covering sharp edges of tin. Nail another piece, forming a 90-degree angle. Repeat for other three corners. Measure the length across the top edge of the longest sides, and cut two pieces of moulding. Nail in place. Repeat for other sides. Note: It might be a good idea to nail boards around underside of box also, as edge is very sharp. Paint trim with acrylic primer.

4. Mix gray and silver paint to match tin and paint boards. Dry-brush dark gray paint over boards and tin; let dry.

5. Coat trim and tile with a thin coat of matte varnish; let dry.

Cactus Rose Planter Box

Materials

8" x 24" piece of $^3/4$"-thick wood
Two cactus-shaped vases 8" high with a 2"-diameter base
Gray and rust acrylic paints
Wood primer
Wood deck sealer
Fine-grain sandpaper
Paintbrushes
Hammer and nails
Drill with 1" and 2" hole saw bits
Saw

Instructions

1. From wood, cut two 9$^3/4$" x 3$^1/2$" pieces for top and bottom and two 11$^1/4$" x 3$^1/2$" pieces for sides.

2. On top piece, center and drill a 1" hole, 2$^5/8$" in from each end. On bottom piece, center and drill a 2" hole about $^3/8$" deep and 2$^5/8$" in from each end.

3. Nail top and bottom between side pieces.

4. Paint frame with wood primer and let dry. Paint frame rust and let dry. Thin gray paint with water, and wash over frame, wiping off any excess paint. When dry, distress frame by sanding. Paint with deck sealer.

5. Vases should set in holes in bottom of frame. Insert flowers through top holes down into vases.

Experiment with different shapes of vases. Try pear-shaped, test tube, or multi-sided vases. Remember, however, to drill holes in bottom to fit vases.

Marbleized Planter Boxes

Materials for two planters

38" x 45" piece of 3/4"-thick wood

Black, blue, cream, metallic gold, emerald-green, moss-green, and white acrylic paints

Wood primer

Wood deck sealer

Paper towels

Fine-grain sandpaper

Paintbrushes

Hammer and nails

Scroll saw

Drill with 1/16" bit

Instructions

Other planter photo on page 144.

1. Enlarge patterns. Transfer patterns to wood and cut out.

2. Nail sides between front and back pieces of each box. Drop bottom down inside box and nail in place. Sand as needed. Drill a few drainage holes in bottom of box.

3. Paint boxes with wood primer; let dry. Paint one box emerald-green, and marbleize with blue, cream, and moss-green; see general instructions on page 10. Paint other box black, and marbleize with white and metallic gold. When dry, coat boxes with deck sealer; let dry.

PLANTER BOX PATTERNS

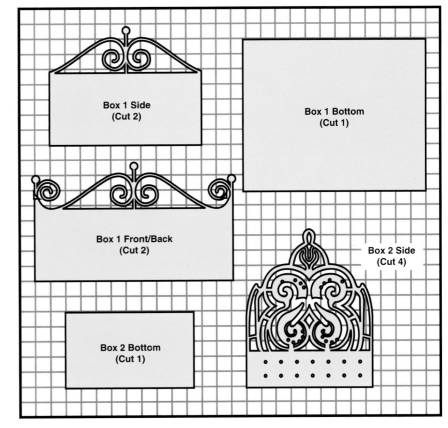

ONE SQUARE EQUALS ONE INCH

Picket Fence Planter Box

Materials

40" x 8" piece of $^3/_8$"-thick wood
20" x 10" piece of $^1/_2$"-thick wood
Scraps of mesh ribbon
Blue, rust, and yellow acrylic paints
Fine-tip permanent black marker
Wood primer
Wood deck sealer
Découpage glue
8$^1/_2$" x 11" sheets of typing paper
Paintbrushes
Hammer and nails
Saw

Instructions

1. Cut 26 pickets from $^3/_8$"-thick wood, following Diagram A on page 93.

2. Cut bottom slats and framing pieces from $^1/_2$"-thick wood, following Diagram A on page 93.

3. For short sides of planter, place two 5$^1/_2$" x 1" pieces horizontally on work surface about 4" apart. Wedge a 4" x 1" piece in at each side to form a frame. Nail in place. Repeat for other side.

4. Nail a 19$^1/_8$" strip between both side frames at top and bottom on both sides. Nail bottom slats into bottom about $^1/_2$" apart, placing the 1$^1/_8$" slats first and last and the 1$^1/_2$" slats in between; see Diagram B.

5. Nail the pickets across the front and back, lining them up with the bottom slats; see Diagram C. Nail three pickets to each side; see Diagram D.

This birdhouse is a perfect accompaniment for the Picket Fence Planter Box. See the Who Me? What Bird? box on page 50 for construction. Color and découpage as with the Picket Fence Planter Box on this page.

6. Paint planter with wood primer and let dry. Thin blue paint with water, and wash color over planter.

7. Create different patterns on paper, using thinned-down shades of blue and yellow, and rust. Try plaids, stripes, and polka dots; refer to photo. When dry, cut patterns into 1$^1/_2$"-wide strips of various lengths. Découpage strips to front of pickets. Pieces of mesh ribbon may also be added to create texture.

8. When planter has dried, transfer drawings of sun and birds on page 92 onto planter with black fine-tip marker.

9. Coat with deck sealer.

PICKET FENCE PLANTER DIAGRAMS

DIAGRAM A

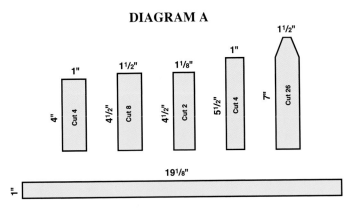

19 1/8"

1"

DIAGRAM B

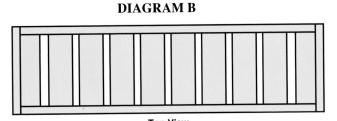

Top View

DIAGRAM C

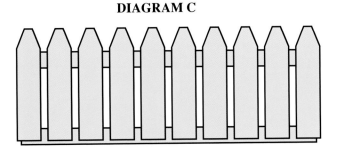

DIAGRAM D

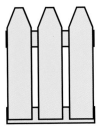

Special Delivery

Materials
Five inexpensive metal mailboxes with posts
Five clay pots that will fit into mailbox opening
One pint each of five colors of satin latex paint
Acrylic primer/sealer
Elastic and reflective roof coating
Wood primer
Small can satin varnish
Deck water sealer
Paint thinner
Paintbrushes

Instructions
Photo on page 5.
1. Paint inside and outside of mailboxes with acrylic primer.

2. Paint mailbox posts with wood primer. Let dry. Paint inside of pots with roof coating and outside of pots with acrylic primer.

3. Paint each mailbox, post, and pot rim a different color. Paint mailbox flag a coordinating color. Two coats may be required on mailbox and post.

4. Varnish mailbox with two thin coats of varnish.

5. Paint posts with deck sealer.

6. Fill pots with dirt and a hanging plant. Lay pot on its side, and wedge into mailbox opening.

Every Bloomin' Neighborhood

Materials

48" x 36" piece of $^3/_4$"-thick pine
Dollhouse trim
Two $2^3/_4$"-square dollhouse windows with shutters
One 3" x 5" dollhouse window with shutters
Two $3^1/_2$" x 8" dollhouse doors
Two 1"-diameter wooden balls
Two $1^1/_2$"-diameter wooden balls
Two wooden egg shapes cut in half
One 2" clay pot cut in half
Country-blue, brown, burgundy, cream, light gray, gray,
  hunter-green, light green, moss-green, navy, dark pink,
  light pink, and white acrylic paints
Acrylic primer
Wood deck sealer
Wood glue
Fine-grain sandpaper
Nails
Paintbrushes
Sponge
Hammer
Saw

Instructions

1. Cut out wood patterns according to diagram.

2. Construct box by nailing side pieces between front and back pieces. Drop bottom inside of box and nail in place. Attach rooftops with wood glue.

3. Paint box with acrylic primer. Let dry. Paint one house and side light gray with gray roof. Paint other house and side cream with navy roof.

4. Position windows and doors in place, and trace areas which will show through. Remove windows and doors, and paint drapes and backgrounds as desired. Paint two smaller windows and one door burgundy and other window and door country-blue. Glue doors and windows in place.

5. Cut away a small portion from wooden balls to create a flat edge. Paint balls and egg-shape halves hunter-green. Paint clay pot halves gray. Position clay pots on each side of burgundy door, and draw a tree trunk coming out of pot. Remove pots and paint trunks brown.

6. Sponge-paint white accents onto gray pots. Sponge-paint light green and moss-green onto ball and half-egg shapes. Paint small dark pink circles onto half-egg shapes. Paint small light pink swirls in dark pink circles.

7. Glue egg-shape halves to side of blue door, forming bushes. Glue pots and wooden balls in place on each side of burgundy door, forming trees; see photo.

8. Cut trim to edge rooftops as desired. Paint to coordinate with houses; let dry. Coat planter with deck sealer.

DIAGRAM

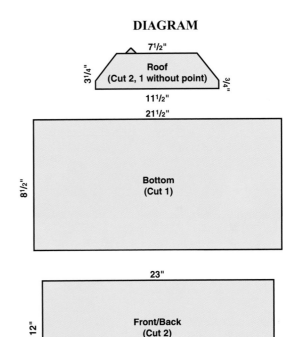

Roof
(Cut 2, 1 without point)
$7^1/_2$"
$3^1/_4$"
$^3/_4$"
$11^1/_2$"

$21^1/_2$"
Bottom
(Cut 1)
$8^1/_2$"

23"
Front/Back
(Cut 2)
12"

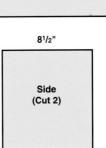

$8^1/_2$"
Side
(Cut 2)
12"

Polka-Dot Pot Planter

Materials

15" x 20" piece of $3/8$"-thick wood
One 1"-diameter stick, $19^1/2$" long
Four $4^1/2$" clay pots
Light brown, light peach, light green, and green acrylic paints
Wood primer
Acrylic primer/sealer
Wood deck sealer
Elastic and reflective roof coating
Fine-grain sandpaper
Paintbrushes
Hammer and nails
Saw

Instructions

1. Enlarge planter side pattern. Transfer pattern to wood and cut out. Also from wood, cut two 20" x 4" pieces for front and back and cut one $19^1/4$" x $5^3/4$" piece for bottom. Sand edges as needed.

2. Nail side pieces between front and back pieces. Drop bottom piece inside and nail in place.

3. Wedge stick handle between side pieces at top and nail in place.

4. Paint box with wood primer and let dry. Paint light brown. When dry, coat with wood deck sealer.

5. Paint inside of pots with roof coating. Let dry. Paint outside of pots with acrylic primer. Let dry.

6. Paint each pot a different color with a coordinating rim. When dry, paint contrasting polka dots.

7. Coat pots with wood deck sealer.

PLANTER SIDE PATTERN

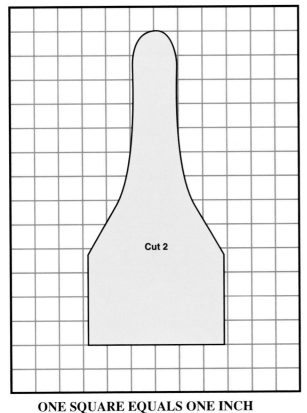

Cut 2

ONE SQUARE EQUALS ONE INCH

VEGETABLE PATTERN

**INSTRUCTIONS FOR VEGETABLE
GARDEN PAIL ON PAGE 98
ENLARGE PATTERN TO FIT PAIL**

Vegetable Garden Pail

Materials

Large metal pail
Two wooden flower cutouts
1 yard of medium-weight wire
Dark green, green, orange, purple, red, and yellow enamel paints
Matte spray varnish
Paintbrushes
Drill with 1/16" bit
Photocopy machine

Instructions

1. Using photocopy machine, enlarge tomato pattern on page 101 to fit pail. Transfer pattern onto pail and paint as shown. Paint one flower red and one purple. When dry, paint a yellow flower center on red flower and a green flower center on purple flower.

2. Drill a hole at top of each flower. Cut wire in half and thread one length through each hole. Twist and curl ends.

3. Spray all items with varnish. Attach flowers to pail handle.

Flowerpot With Birdhouse Picks

Materials

One 4"-tall terra-cotta pot with saucer
Two miniature birdhouses
Two small wooden bird cutouts
One small wooden tulip cutout
16" length of 3/16"-diameter wooden dowel
Spanish moss
Pale blue, blue, green, red, off-white, and yellow acrylic paints
Acrylic primer/sealer
Elastic and reflective roof coating
Wood deck sealer
Industrial-strength glue
Paintbrushes
Drill with 3/16" bit

Instructions

1. Coat inside of pot with roof coating; coat outside of pot and saucer with acrylic primer; let dry. Paint pot rim, saucer, and front and back of birdhouses with two to three coats of off-white paint.

2. Paint bottom and sides of pot and the base of one birdhouse with two to three coats of yellow paint. Let dry. Lightly draw a checkerboard design around the rim of the pot and the saucer; see photo on opposite page. Paint every other square pale blue. Also, paint the sides and base of remaining birdhouse pale blue. Paint tulip, roof of blue birdhouse, and perch on yellow birdhouse red; let dry. Paint birds and roof of yellow birdhouse blue.

3. Cut a 7 1/2" piece and a 8 1/2" length from wooden dowel. Paint the dowels and the perch on blue birdhouse green. Paint the details onto the birds and birdhouses; see photo.

4. Drill a hole in the center bottom of each birdhouse. Glue one dowel into each hole. Coat all pieces with deck sealer; let dry. Glue tulip and birds to front of pot; see photo. Glue moss in birdhouse doors.

Summer Frost Snowflake Pot

Break It To Me Gently

A Home For All Seasons

Variations On A Theme

Summer Frost Snowflake Pot

Break It To Me Gently

Materials

Clay pot with saucer
Old strips of lace
Masking tape
Pale blue acrylic paint
Flat white spray paint
Temporary spray adhesive
Acrylic primer/sealer
Elastic and reflective roof coating
Wood deck sealer
Paintbrushes
Sponge
Photocopy machine

LEAF PATTERN

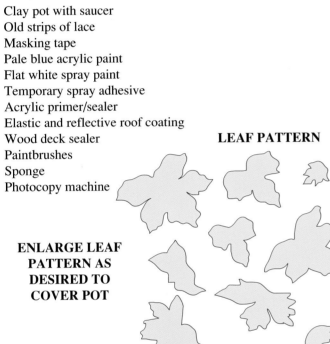

ENLARGE LEAF PATTERN AS DESIRED TO COVER POT

Instructions

1. Coat inside of pot with roof coating; coat outside of pot and saucer with acrylic sealer; let dry. Using photocopy machine, enlarge pattern as desired. Transfer leaf pattern onto pot. Paint leaves with thinned pale blue paint. Paint stems connecting leaves together to create vines.

2. Mask off top rim of pot. Place pot upside down and spray with temporary adhesive. Press lace strips into place, overlapping as to not leave any gaps. Note: The last strip will need to be cut triangular to fit pot. Spray over lace with white paint. Remove lace. Cover finished part of pot with paper, and repeat process on rim.

3. Sponge-paint saucer with pale blue paint. When completely dry, coat pot and saucer with deck sealer.

Materials

Clay pot with saucer
Broken plates
One tube of tub-and-tile silicone caulking
White sanded grout
Elastic and reflective roof coating
Wood deck sealer
Paintbrushes
Craft stick
Brown paper sack
Two towels
Damp rag
Hammer

Instructions

1. Place plates in a brown paper sack between two towels. Strike with hammer, breaking plates. Continue until plates are broken into roughly 1" pieces.

2. Place a dab of caulking on the back of a piece of broken plate. Press onto pot. Continue placing pieces onto pot, leaving about 1/4" of space between each piece. Be careful when working with glass. Very sharp edges should be filed off.

3. Mix sanded grout, following manufacturer's instructions. The easiest way to press grout between the pieces is with your finger, but a craft stick may be used. Place grout heavily around pieces and press, working small areas at a time. Go over grouted areas with a damp rag. Continue until pot is covered. Let dry.

4. Paint inside of pot with coating; coat outside of pot with deck sealer.

Instead of plates, try using marbles, tiles, jewels, or small momentos.

A Home For All Seasons

Materials

Large clay pot and saucer
Black, medium blue, dark blue, medium brown, medium
    green, dark green, off-white, and red acrylic paints
Wood deck sealer
Elastic and reflective roof coating
Fine-tip permanent black marker
Calligraphy-tip permanent black marker
Natural sponge
Paintbrushes
Photocopy machine

Instructions

1. Coat inside of pot with roof coating; let dry.

2. Using a photocopy machine, enlarge house and tree patterns 200%. Transfer patterns to the center front of pot; see photo. Do not transfer details such as doors, windows, etc.

3. Paint house with a base coat of medium blue; paint roof and trees medium brown. Let dry.

4. Transfer details to house. Paint, referring to pattern. Let dry.

5. Outline shapes with black marker.

6. Using sponge, paint grass and leaves on trees dark green. Sponge-paint lightly over top of dark green with medium green paint. When dry, paint a few red apples in trees.

7. Using a permanent calligraphy marker, write family name across top of pot.

8. Paint entire pot with deck sealer.

HOUSE & TREE PATTERNS

ENLARGE PATTERNS 200%

Variations On A Theme

Materials
Three various sized clay pots
Lime-green, green, pink, red, and white acrylic paints
Wood deck sealer
Elastic and reflective roof coating
Paintbrushes
Sponge
Photocopy machine

Instructions
1. Coat inside of pots with roof coating; let dry. Sponge-paint around rim of pots with lime-green and green paint.

2. Using photocopy machine, enlarge pattern below to fit various sized pots. Transfer pattern onto pot and paint according to pattern. When dry, paint outside of pots with deck sealer.

FLOWERPOT PATTERN

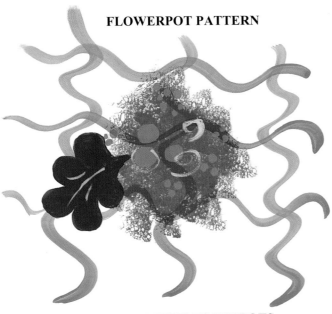

ENLARGE PATTERN TO FIT POTS

Boot Planters

Materials
1 pair of rubber galoshes
Plants or flowers

Instructions
Plant flowers in galoshes.

Try using an assortment of different types of boots to create an entire boot garden.

Farmer's Market

Materials

6"-tall clay pot with saucer
Black, green, light green, and red acrylic paints
Acrylic primer/sealer
Wood deck sealer
Elastic and reflective roof coating
Paintbrushes

Instructions

1. Coat inside of pot with roof coating. Coat outside of pot and saucer with acrylic primer.

2. Paint outside of pot red. Let dry. Paint saucer green.

3. Paint bottom and 1" up side of pot green. Using the dry-brush technique, paint a 1" area above green paint light green. Paint black seeds throughout red area; see pattern.

4. When dry, paint outside of pot and saucer with deck sealer.

WATERMELON PATTERN

A Perennial Pumpkin Patch

Materials

6"-tall clay pot with saucer
Black, green, light green, and orange acrylic paints
Acrylic primer/sealer
Wood deck sealer
Elastic and reflective roof coating
Paintbrushes

Instructions

1. Coat inside of pot with roof coating. Coat outside of pot and saucer with acrylic primer.

2. Paint outside of pot and saucer orange. Let dry.

3. Transfer pattern onto pot. Paint eyes, nose, and mouth black. Paint leaves and vine green; accent with light green.

4. When dry, paint outside of pot and saucer with deck sealer.

PUMPKIN PATTERN

Two-Tiered Plant Stand

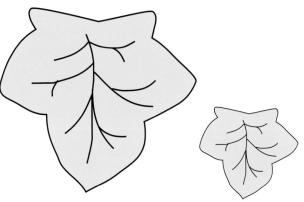

Materials

One two-tiered wrought-iron plant stand
Two clay pots to fit stand
18" of 14-gauge copper wire
3 yards of 18-gauge copper wire
12" square of 36-gauge tooling copper
Four clusters of gold grapes
Gold wrapping paper with fruit design
One sheet of gold leafing
Soft cloth
Green and maroon acrylic paints
Metallic copper spray paint
Gold leaf adhesive
Découpage glue
Acrylic primer/sealer
Elastic and reflective roof coating
Matte varnish
Pencil
Paintbrush
Sponge brush
Needle-nose pliers
Wire cutters
Tin snips or an old pair of scissors
Soldering iron and solder

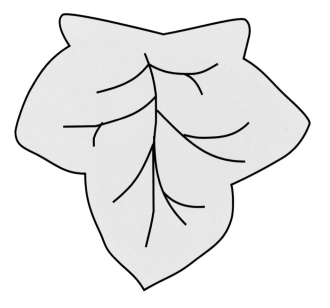

With right side up, place copper on a stack of paper. Emboss veins onto leaves, according to patterns; see general instructions for embossing on page 11. Wipe away any residue with soft cloth. Cut out leaves.

Instructions

1. Paint inside of pots with roof coating; paint outside with acrylic primer; let dry. Cut wrapping paper to fit around bottom of pots. Découpage paper onto pots. Let dry.

2. Paint around top rim of pots, inside and outside, with gold leaf adhesive and let set up. Press gold leafing onto adhesive. Rub off excess with soft cloth. Coat pots with deck sealer

3. Paint plant stand metallic copper, allowing some of the wrought iron to show through. Let dry.

4. Trace leaf patterns onto tooling copper, making three large leaves, four medium leaves, and 16 small leaves.

5. Cut 18-gauge wire into twenty-three 3" lengths. Solder one wire to the back center of each leaf. Cut remaining wire into 10" lengths, and wrap each around pencil to curl.

6. Starting at top of plant stand, wrap 14-gauge wire down one side and across to bottom of other side. Secure ends onto plant stand with needle-nose pliers.

7. Secure grapes around 14-gauge wire, referring to photo on page 106 for placement. Add leaves and curls as desired, securing ends with needle-nose pliers.

8. Paint over solder marks on leaves with metallic copper paint. Dry-brush green paint onto leaves. Dry-brush maroon paint onto grapes. Coat entire plant stand with matte varnish, following manufacturer's instructions.

The Rabbit In The Hat Trick

ENLARGE PATTERN TO 200%

Materials

One 6$^1/_2$"-diameter clay pot
One 8" x 10" piece of $^3/_4$"-thick wood
Four 1" wooden stars
Three 1$^1/_4$" x $^3/_4$" thin wooden rectangles for cards
3" length of $^3/_{16}$"-diameter dowel
32" of 24-gauge gold wire
Black, blue, metallic gold, pink, red, off-white, and white
 acrylic paints
Acrylic primer/sealer
Elastic and reflective roof coating
Wood deck sealer
Fine-tip permanent black marker
Industrial-strength glue
Paintbrushes
Drill with $^1/_{16}$" and $^3/_{16}$" bits
Saw
Photocopy machine

Instructions

1. Using a photocopy machine, enlarge pattern 200%. Trace rabbit pattern onto wood and cut out. Note: A similar purchased cutout may be used.

2. Paint wood cutout and outside of pot with acrylic sealer; paint inside of pot with roof coating. Let dry.

3. Paint rabbit white and pot black. Let dry.

4. Transfer pattern to rabbit. Paint ears pink and bow tie blue. Paint eyes, nose, and dowel black. When completely dry, draw whiskers, mouth, bow tie outline, and ear outline with black marker.

5. Using the $^1/_{16}$" bit, drill one hole in each star. Paint stars metallic gold.

6. Paint one side of each rectangle off-white and the other side black. Paint red hearts and diamond, and black club onto cards.

7. Spray pot and all wood pieces with deck sealer.

8. Cut gold wire into four 8" lengths. Attach a wire into each star through drill hole. Twist wires around paintbrush to curl. Drill a hole into one end of dowel. Glue wires into dowel hole. With $^3/_{16}$" bit, drill a hole in one of rabbit's paws. Glue dowel into hole.

9. Glue cards together; see photo. Glue to rabbit's other paw. Glue rabbit to top back edge of pot. Coat inside of pot.

Three Hanging Flowerpots

Materials

Three 4" clay pots
One 3" wooden finial with a $1/2$"-diameter hole in bottom
One 1" wood screw
Two yards of $1/4$" decorative cording
Printed tissue paper
Three colors of acrylic paint to match tissue paper
Découpage glue
Acrylic primer/sealer
Elastic and reflective roof coating
Wood deck sealer
Paintbrushes
Screwdriver

Instructions

1. Paint inside of each pot with roof coating. Let dry. Paint each pot lip with acrylic primer; let dry. Paint each pot lip and top 2" inside each pot a coordinating color.

2. Découpage tissue paper to sides and bottom of pots and wooden finial. Let dry. When dry, apply a second coat of glue; let dry. Note: It is helpful to tear tissue paper into small pieces when covering smaller, detailed areas.

3. Coat all surfaces with deck sealer; let dry.

4. Fold cording in half and slide screw into center. Use screwdriver and insert screw into hole in finial. Tie an overhand knot, and thread both ends of cording up through hole in bottom of one pot. Pull until finial rests securely on bottom of pot. Tie a square knot in the bottom, and thread on second pot. Mark position with a pin, slide pot off, and tie a square knot at pin mark. Thread pot back on and repeat for last pot. Tie ends together for hanging.

Sweet Honeybee Flowerpot

Sweet Honeybee Flowerpot

Materials

One clay pot with saucer (model is 9$^1/_2$")
Golden-tan and pale yellow acrylic paints
Transfer paper
Elastic and reflective roof coating
Wood deck sealer
Paintbrushes
Photocopy machine

Instructions

1. Paint inside of pot with roof coating; let dry.

2. Using photocopy machine, enlarge honeycomb patterns 200%. Transfer pattern onto clay pot. Place bees randomly throughout honeycomb.

3. Paint honeycomb with pale yellow, inverting pattern on rim as in photo. Paint bees with golden-tan. Thin golden-tan with water, and paint wings to give transparent appearance. Paint a line under edge of rim and around ridge of saucer with pale yellow.

4. When completely dry, cover pot with deck sealer.

HONEYCOMB PATTERNS

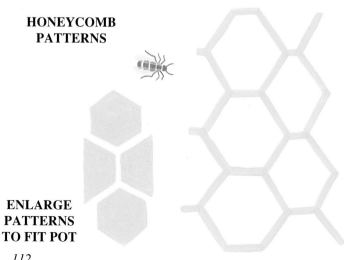

ENLARGE PATTERNS TO FIT POT

Garden Butterfly Plant Markers

Materials

12" square of $^3/_4$"-thick wood
Three 1-yard lengths of $^1/_4$"-diameter wooden dowel
Six corsage pins
Acrylic paints in desired colors
Découpage glue
Wood glue
Wood deck sealer
Paintbrushes
Saw
Drill with $^1/_4$" bit
Color photocopy machine

Instructions

1. Using a color photocopy machine, enlarge patterns on page 114 to 125%, making two copies of each. Transfer patterns to wood and cut out butterfly shapes.

2. Drill holes in bottom of butterflies to insert dowels.

3. Paint sides of butterflies in desired color. Paint dowels as desired.

4. Cut out color copies and découpage to front and back of butterflies. Apply several coats of glue.

5. Push pins in position as "antennae." Glue dowels into butterflies. Coat markers with deck sealer.

You may choose to paint desired vegetables onto wood instead of découpaging color copies. For example, beans, tomatoes, peas, and so forth. Draw words and details with a black marker.

Garden Butterfly Plant Markers

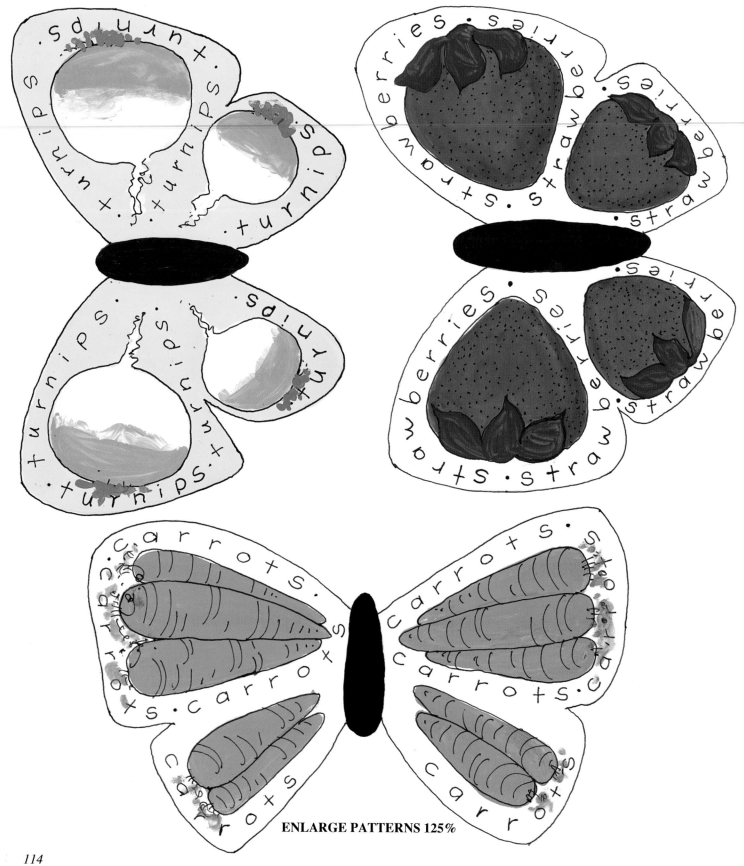

ENLARGE PATTERNS 125%

114

A Bird Of A Different Feather

Materials

One 6"-square piece of $3/4$"-thick wood
One clay pot with saucer
$1/2$" x $3/4$" piece of wood, 16" long
1" grabber screw
Black, green, orange, red, rust, tan, and yellow acrylic paints
Acrylic primer/sealer
Wood deck sealer
Elastic and reflective roof coating
Toothbrush
Paintbrushes
Saw
Photocopy machine

ROOSTER PATTERN

ENLARGE PATTERN 205%

Instructions

1. Using a photocopy machine, enlarge rooster pattern 205%. Trace pattern onto tracing paper. Place graphite paper on 6" wood square and lay pattern on top. Trace pattern onto wood. Cut shape and sand edges.

2. Cut one end of 16" length of wood into a point. Coat inside of pot with roof coating. Paint all wood pieces, outside of pot, and saucer with acrylic primer. Let dry. Paint 16" length of wood and pot green. Paint rooster according to pattern.

3. Attach 16" length to back of wooden cutout with grabber screw; see photo. Using a toothbrush, splatter rooster with tan paint and pot with rust paint; let dry. Coat all pieces with deck sealer. Let dry.

Farm-Animals Hose Guards

Materials

Three 6"-square pieces of ³/₄"-thick wood
Three ¹/₂" x ³/₄" pieces of wood, 16" long
Three 1" grabber screws
Black, dark green, light green, orange, dark pink, light pink, red, dark tan, light tan, white, and yellow acrylic paints
Wood primer
Wood deck sealer
Toothbrush
Saw
Photocopy machine

Instructions

1. Using a photocopy machine, enlarge animal patterns 145%. Trace patterns onto tracing paper. Place graphite paper on 6" wood squares and lay patterns on top. Trace patterns onto wood. Cut shapes and sand edges.

2. Cut one end of each 16" length of wood into a point.

3. Coat all wood pieces with wood primer. Let dry.

4. Paint according to pattern and photo; let dry between coats.

5. Attach 16" lengths to backs of wooden cutouts with grabber screws; see photo.

6. Using a toothbrush, splatter all wood pieces with dark tan paint; let dry.

7. Coat all wood pieces with deck sealer. Let dry.

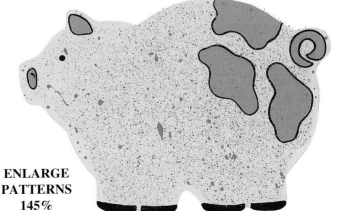

ENLARGE PATTERNS 145%

Marble Finial Hose Guards

Materials

Two egg-shaped ornamental finials
Two 14" lengths of 1"-diameter wooden dowel
Two double-threaded screws
Two metal spikes
Beige, metallic gold, light gray, light green, off-white, and
    light yellow acrylic paints
Acrylic primer/sealer
Wood deck sealer
Paintbrushes
Paper towels
Drill

Instructions

1.   Drill holes for screws in one end of each dowel and in both finial flat ends.

2.   Coat all pieces with acrylic primer; let dry. Paint top of egg shapes with off-white paint and let dry. Dip damp paper towel into light yellow paint and blot sparingly onto eggs. Repeat with beige and light gray. Thin a small amount of off-white paint with water, and repeat paper towel process on top of other colors. Let dry.

3.   With fine brush, paint squiggly lines onto top of eggs with light green, light yellow, and light gray paint.

4.   Paint dowels and bottom portion of finials light green. Let dry.

5.   Using dry-brush technique, brush metallic gold over light green on dowels and finials. Screw finials onto dowels. Paint hose guards with deck sealer; let dry.

6.   Insert metal spikes into bottom of dowels. Note: Instead of using metal spikes, cut end of dowel to a point.

Oriental-Style Hose Guards

Materials

Two wooden finials with one pointed end
Two 14" lengths of 1"-diameter wooden dowel
Two double-threaded screws
Two metal spikes
Four bugle beads
Four 2mm beads
Four straight pins
Beige, black, gold, green, rust, and off-white acrylic paints
Acrylic primer/sealer
Wood deck sealer
Paintbrushes
Small sponge
Drill

Instructions

1. Drill holes for screws in one end of each dowel and in both finial flat ends. Coat all pieces with acrylic primer; let dry.

2. For Oriental woman, paint facial area beige, hair (point included) black, and dress off-white with a rust hem. Thin rust, gold, and green paint with water, and sponge flowers and leaves onto dress. With liner brush, paint eyes, nose, and mouth black. For Oriental man, paint facial area beige, hair black, hat rust, body gold. Sponge gold paint lightly onto hat. Sponge rust and green paint lightly onto body. With liner brush, paint eyes, nose, and mouth black.

3. Thread a 2mm bead and a bugle bead onto each straight pin. Push pins into top of woman's head for hair pins.

4. Screw painted finials onto dowels. Paint dowels and bottoms of finials black. Let dry. Paint hose guards with deck sealer; let dry. Insert metal spikes into bottoms of dowels. Note: Instead of using metal spikes, cut end of dowel to a point.

"Garden Of Friends" Picket Fence

Materials

24" x 14" piece of $1/4$"-thick plywood
Black, light brown, green, gold and off-white acrylic paints
Wood primer
Matte spray sealer
Fine-tip permanent black marker
Paintbrushes
Hammer and nails
Saw
Photocopy machine

Instructions

1. Using photocopy machine, enlarge flower and picket patterns 400%. From wood, cut one bird picket, five pickets without bird, and two 1" x 24" pieces for braces.

2. Assemble fence by positioning 1" x 24" pieces horizontally about $3^1/2$" apart for braces. Nail pickets vertically across braces, spaced 2" apart. The bird picket should be first; see diagram.

3. Paint wood with primer and let dry. Thin light brown paint with water. Dip scrunched paper towel into thinned paint and wipe over fence.

4. Transfer flower pattern onto fence. Paint flowers gold with light brown centers, leaves light green, and words and bird black. When completely dry, outline flowers, leaves and fencing with black marker. Spray with matte sealer.

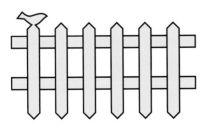

DIAGRAM

Photo on page 7.

FLOWER PATTERN

Plant seeds of Love and your garden of friends will grow.

PICKET PATTERN

ENLARGE PATTERNS 400%

Twig By Twig Posted Fence

Materials

Twigs (8" long and between $1/2$" and $3/4$" diameter)
Heavy wire (double the desired length of fence)
Wire cutters
Drill with $1/8$" bit
Saw

Instructions

Photo on page 7.

The amount of twigs used will determine how long the fence is. All twigs should be about the same length and diameter.

1. Drill a hole about $1^1/2$" down from top end of each twig. Drill a second hole about 4" down from first hole.

2. Run lengths of wire through drill holes to connect twigs. Work small sections at a time, leaving wire long enough to connect next section.

"Welcome To Our Pad" Pool Stakes

Materials for three stakes

Three 8" x 21" pieces of ³/₈"-thick wood
Green, orange, hot-pink, purple, and white acrylic paints
Wood primer
Wood deck sealer
Paintbrushes
Fine-grain sandpaper
Saw
Photocopy machine

Instructions

1. Using a photocopy machine, enlarge frog patterns 200%. Transfer patterns to top edge of each wood piece, centered side to side. Continue to trace vertical lines at the bottom of each frog the length of the wood. Cut stakes from wood. Cut each stake end at a point.

2. Sand edges and paint with wood primer.

3. Paint with acrylic paints according to patterns.

4. When completely dry, coat with deck sealer.

FROG PATTERNS

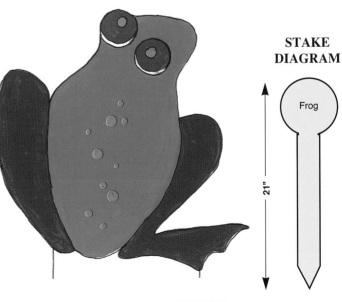

STAKE DIAGRAM

Frog

21"

ENLARGE PATTERNS 200%

Plant A Beach Party

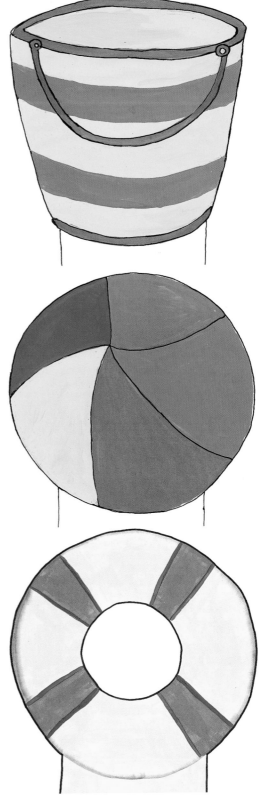

Materials

Four 8" x 21" pieces of $^3/_8$"-thick wood
Blue, green, orange, pink, off-white and yellow acrylic paints
Wood primer
Wood deck sealer
Paintbrushes
Fine-grain sandpaper
Saw
Photocopy machine

Instructions

1. Using a photocopy machine, enlarge beach patterns 200%. Transfer patterns to top edge of each wood piece, centered side to side. Continue to trace vertical lines at the bottom of each pattern the length of the wood. Cut stakes from wood. Cut each stake end at a point.

2. Sand edges and paint with wood primer.

3. Paint with acrylic paints according to patterns.

4. When completely dry, coat with deck sealer.

**STAKE
DIAGRAM**

Pattern

21"

ENLARGE PATTERNS 200%

Jubilation

Swing Into Summer Fun

Materials

One discarded swing set (model has a horse, swings, and glider)
Four metal plant hangers
Four clay pots for plant hangers
Three clay pots for planter box
One wooden planter box made to fit glider
Two screw hangers
One pint each of six colors satin latex paint
Wood primer
Elastic and reflective roof coating
Acrylic primer/sealer
Wood deck sealer
Small can satin spread varnish
Paint thinner
Paintbrushes
New pencil with eraser
Saw
Hammer and nails
Drill

Invigorate an old swing set like the one above with fresh paint and flowers. The finished photo is on page 126.

Instructions

1. Remove swings, horse, and glider from swing set. Discard swings but save chains.

2. Drill a hole at each end of top bar and insert screw hangers.

3. Paint swing set, glider, and chains with acrylic primer. Paint swing set one solid color. Paint glider and chains desired color.

4. Dip eraser end of pencil into lighter-colored paint, and add polka dots to most of the poles on swing set.

5. Paint horse and saddle in desired colors, following established pattern on horse. Let paint dry between colors. Paint polka dots on horse's saddle, as in Step 4.

6. Build or purchase a planter box to the dimensions that will fit into glider. Paint planter box with wood primer inside and out. Paint planter box as desired. When dry, coat planter box with deck sealer.

7. Brush the insides of all pots with roof coating. Paint outside of four pots with acrylic primer; let dry. Paint these four pots each with a different color. Paint rims, both inside and out, with a coordinating color. When dry, add polka dots to two of the painted pots, as in Step 4. When dry, paint the outside of the four pots with deck sealer. Plant as desired.

8. Brush two coats of satin varnish on swing set, glider, and horse. Let dry. Hang two metal plant hangers from chains in center of swing set, and insert two of the painted pots. Hang other plant hangers on each end of the swing set, and insert painted pots.

9. Place planter box in position in glider, and insert unpainted pots into planter.

Natural Solutions

Materials

Two 30"-diameter clay pots
Pre-form concrete slab for tabletop
Submersible pump
Several bricks
Acrylic paints in desired colors
Cement mix
Clear quick-drying caulking
Acrylic primer/sealer
Elastic and reflective roof coating
Wood deck sealer
Paintbrushes

Instructions

1. Paint the inside of both pots with roof coating.

2. Place the pump in one pot, and pull cord through drainage hole. Note: Hole may need to be enlarged with drill to fit plug through. Keep enough cord inside of pot for pump to set on several bricks. Mix cement, following manufacturer's instructions. Plug hole, securing cord, with cement; let dry. Caulk around hole to prevent leaking; let dry. Place three bricks under pump in center of pot.

3. Coat outside of pots and concrete slab with acrylic primer; let dry. Paint outside of pots and concrete slab as desired with acrylic paints; let dry. Coat all surfaces with deck sealer.

4. Fill the first pot with water to the desired level. Do not let the water level dip below the pump.

5. Place concrete slab on top of other pot for table.

Ruby Begonia

Materials

Clay pots in the following quantities and sizes:
  three 4^1/$_2$", ten 2", two 2^3/$_4$", two 2^1/$_2$", and six 1^1/$_2$"
One 7^1/$_2$" clay saucer
One wooden flower cutout
Small white basket
15" length of ^{10}/$_{24}$" threaded rod
Two 7" lengths of ^{1}/$_4$" threaded rod
Four ^{1}/$_4$" nuts
Four ^{10}/$_{24}$" nuts
Eight beads with ^{1}/$_4$" centers
18" of heavy wire
Black, blue, brown, green, peach, red, white, and
  yellow acrylic paints
Wood deck sealer
Elastic and reflective roof coating
All-purpose cement glue
Paintbrushes
Two pairs of pliers
Drill with ^{3}/$_8$" and ^{1}/$_2$" bits
Photocopy machine

Instructions

1. With ^{1}/$_2$" bit, carefully drill two holes in the bottom of the clay saucer, one on each side. Drill two holes in the bottom of one 4^1/$_2$" pot, one on each side of the drainage hole. With ^{3}/$_8$" bit, drill two holes on each side of another 4^1/$_2$" pot about 1" up from bottom. Paint inside of remaining 4 ^{1}/$_2$" pot with roof coating. Paint outside of all pots and saucer with acrylic primer; let dry.

2. Paint the two 4^1/$_2$" pots with drill holes red with white polka dots. Paint other 4^1/$_2$" pot peach with red rim. Paint ten 2" pots red with white polka dots. Paint six 1^1/$_2$" pots white. Paint two 2^1/$_2$" pots white. Paint two 2^3/$_4$" pots white with red rims. Paint clay saucer green. Paint wooden flower yellow with brown center and brown highlights. Let dry completely.

FACE PATTERN

ENLARGE PATTERN 140%

3. Invert clay saucer and run ^{1}/$_4$" threaded rods through drill holes. These will be the legs. Screw a nut on each rod inside of saucer. Layer one 2^3/$_4$", one 2^1/$_2$", and three 1^1/$_2$" pots on each rod. Insert end of rods through drill holes in bottom of 4^1/$_2$" pot, and screw nuts on ends inside of pot.

4. Insert ^{10}/$_{24}$" threaded rod through side drill holes in 4^1/$_2$" pot. Thread a nut onto each end of rod and screw up to edge of pot. Invert pot so that arms are at the top. Hold the base of one arm with pliers, and grasp end with second pair of pliers. Bend rod so that it points upward. Layer five 2" pots onto rod, inserting a bead between each one. Thread a nut onto end of rod in last pot. Repeat for other arm, bending it forward. Paint protruding portion of rod and nut red.

5. Using photocopy machine, enlarge face pattern 140%. Paint face onto peach pot with red rim.

6. Glue upper body to bottom half with all-purpose cement. Glue head to upper body.

7. Drill a hole in one side of wooden flower. Insert wire into hole and twist. Curl wire and stick in top pot. Glue small basket onto one arm.

8. Paint entire project with deck sealer.

DIAGRAM

Gardening Lady

Materials

Two 72" x 48" pieces of $^3/_4$" wood
48" of $^1/_2$"-diameter rebar
Two 2" eye screws
Two hinges with screws
About 40 flat-sided rhinestones in assorted colors
One package of ladybug "Jewels" with flat sides
Four miniature garden tools
48" of 1"-wide gold ribbon
Black, several shades of green, orange, peach, purple, red, and
    yellow acrylic paints
Wood primer
Wood deck sealer
Industrial-strength glue
Fishing line or nylon thread
Paintbrushes
Drill with $^1/_2$" bit
Hammer and nails
Saw

Instructions

1. Enlarge gardening lady patterns on page 135. Transfer patterns to wood. Cut out shapes.

2. Assemble planter box by nailing side pieces between front and back pieces. Drop bottom inside box and nail in place. Assemble stand in same manner, excluding bottom; top will lay on top of stand box. Nail in place.

3. Drill a $^3/_4$" hole in top of base behind slot.

4. Paint all wood pieces with wood primer; let dry. Paint gardening lady, arms, base, and flower box according to pattern and color scheme on page 134.

5. Nail flower box to center of figure. Attach arms to shoulders with hinges. Insert eye screws onto back of figure at center back and skirt edge level.

Make a Gardening Lady for each of the holidays. To make the Halloween Witch, cut a hat pattern from wood and nail it to the top of head. Use a Halloween color scheme to decorate. To make the Christmas Angel, cut wings from wood and nail to back. Use a Christmas color scheme to decorate.

6. Insert garden lady into slot in base, and slip rebar through eye screws and into hole in base.

7. Coat entire project with deck sealer.

8. Use industrial-strength glue to attach ladybugs to neck for necklace and on each ear for earrings. Glue a length of fishing line to the handles of miniature garden tools, and hang from each ladybug earring, securing with glue. Glue rhinestones for eyes and at flower centers. Tie two bows with gold ribbon and glue to shoes.

GARDENING LADY PATTERNS

CHRISTMAS

SUMMER

HALLOWEEN

GARDENING LADY PATTERNS

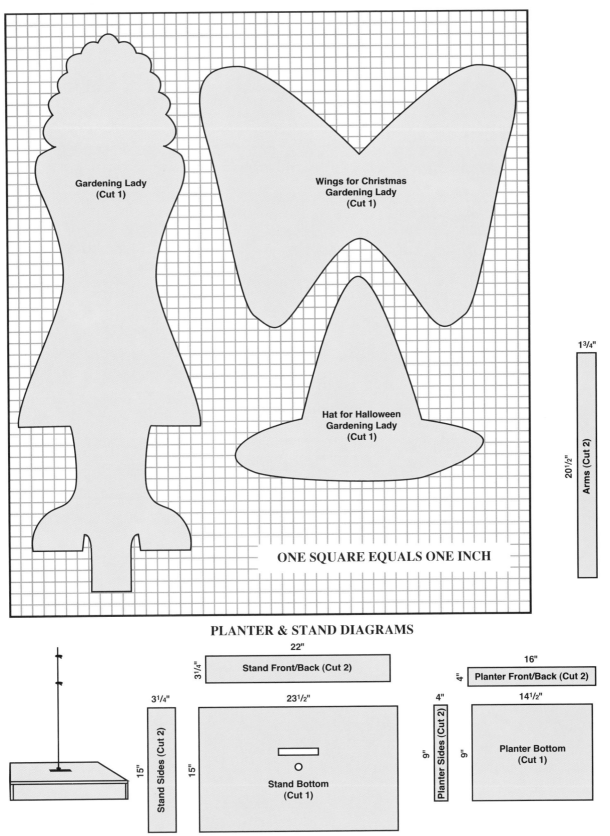

Gardening Lady
(Cut 1)

Wings for Christmas
Gardening Lady
(Cut 1)

Hat for Halloween
Gardening Lady
(Cut 1)

1³/₄"

20¹/₂"

Arms (Cut 2)

ONE SQUARE EQUALS ONE INCH

PLANTER & STAND DIAGRAMS

22"

3¹/₄"

Stand Front/Back (Cut 2)

16"

4"

Planter Front/Back (Cut 2)

3¹/₄"

Stand Sides (Cut 2)

15"

23¹/₂"

15"

Stand Bottom
(Cut 1)

4"

Planter Sides (Cut 2)

9"

9"

14¹/₂"

Planter Bottom
(Cut 1)

I Never Saw A Purple Cow

Materials

24" x 18" piece of $1/2$"-thick wood (Cow can also be cut from heavy metal if desired)
$1^1/2$" x $1^1/2$" x 3" wood block
18" piece of $5/8$"-diameter radiator hose with two clamps
Female hose end
3" length of $3/8$"-diameter copper tubing
1" conduit hole strap with screws
Two metal stakes about 6 to 8" long
Four $1/4$" wood screws, $3/4$" long
One pair of sunglasses
1 yard of 2"-wide pink wired ribbon
Coral, pink, purple, and yellow acrylic paints
Exterior white flat paint
Wood primer
Wood deck sealer
Paintbrushes
Hot glue gun and glue sticks
Pliers
Hammer and nails
Drill with $1/4$" bit

Instructions

1. Enlarge cow patterns. Transfer patterns to wood and cut out.

2. Nail wooden block vertically to front of cow at head position. Nail head onto wooden block.

3. Drill two holes in tops of each metal stake, and position below front and back hoof. Mark drill holes. Drill holes in wood and screw stakes in place with $3/4$"-long wood screws.

4. Screw 1"-diameter clamp onto back of cow at tail position. Insert radiator hose through center of clamp.

On the end of hose behind cow, insert female hose end and clamp in place. Using pliers, smash one end of copper tubing until almost closed, and insert open end in other end of hose. Clamp in place.

5. Paint entire cow with primer. Let dry.

6. Paint entire cow with white flat paint. Let dry.

7. Paint cow with acrylic paints as desired.

8. Apply several coats of outdoor varnish, letting varnish dry thoroughly between coats.

9. Remove sides from sunglasses. Hot-glue in place. Press cow into ground and hook up to garden hose. Turn on water and watch the tail spray!

COW PATTERNS

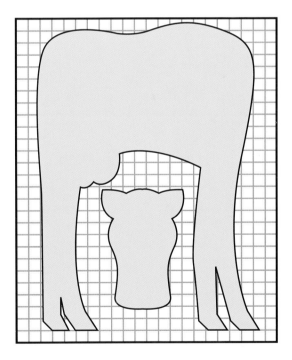

ONE SQUARE EQUALS ONE INCH

"Down to Business" Mr. Scarecrow

Materials

24" x 60" piece of $^3/4$"-thick wood
Four $^1/4$" wing nuts
Four $2^1/4$"-long bolts with washers
12" of lightweight wire
Three $1^1/2$" wood screws
Men's clothing: dress shirt, tie, belt, pants
Briefcase
Toy cellular phone
Play money
Small garbage bag
Newspaper
Yellow contact paper
Safety pins
Black, flesh tone, gray, and white acrylic paints
Acrylic primer/sealer
Wood deck sealer
Paintbrushes
Drill with $^1/4$" bit
Screwdriver
Staple gun
Hand saw

Instructions

1. Enlarge head pattern. Transfer pattern to wood and cut out. Also from wood, cut a $1^1/2$" x 60" piece for body post and four $1^1/2$" x 15" pieces for arms.

2. Drill a hole 1" in from each end of two arm pieces. Drill a hole 1" in from one end of remaining two arm pieces. Drill a hole on each end of shoulders.

3. Paint head piece with acrylic primer and let dry. Paint face and hat according to pattern and let dry. Coat with deck sealer.

4. Lay head piece face down, and attach body post to back of head, using three wood screws. Body post should extend 9" up from shoulders. Using wing nuts, bolts, and washers, attach the upper arm (piece with two drill holes) to one shoulder. Attach the lower arm (piece with one drill hole) at elbow. Repeat for other arm.

5. Slip shirt onto scarecrow, adjust arm position, and tighten wing nuts. Fill small garbage bag with crumpled newspaper, and tie knot at top of bag. Stuff bag inside of shirt, and staple to post about 9" down from neck. Pad shoulders with newspaper. Insert post down one pant leg, and attach pants to waistline with safety pins. Staple back of pants to post. Add belt and tie.

6. Staple play money around neck and arms. Money can be laminated if weather is a concern. Clip pay phone to cuff and wire as needed to secure. Cut "1-800-EAT CROW" from yellow contact paper. Peel and attach letters to briefcase.

HEAD PATTERN

ONE SQUARE EQUALS ONE INCH

Brilliant Sunflower Garden Tray

Instructions

1. Paint tray with wood primer and let dry.

2. Using a photocopy machine, enlarge sunflower pattern to fit tray. Transfer pattern to tray. Paint tray according to pattern. Let dry.

3. Using a fine-tipped brush, paint details with black and orange paint. Spray with acrylic sealer.

Materials

Large, round wooden tray
Black, blue, green, orange, red, white, and yellow
    acrylic paints
Wood primer
Acrylic spray sealer
Paintbrushes
Photocopy machine

Paint flowerpots bright, solid colors matching tray, and place them on brightly painted hanging metal plant holders for a beautiful garden combination.

SUNFLOWER PATTERN

ENLARGE PATTERN TO FIT TRAY

METRIC EQUIVALENCE CHART

MM-Millimetres   CM-Centimetres

INCHES TO MILLIMETRES AND CENTIMETRES

INCHES	MM	CM	INCHES	CM	INCHES	CM
⅛	3	0.3	9	22.9	30	76.2
¼	6	0.6	10	25.4	31	78.7
½	13	1.3	12	30.5	33	83.8
⅝	16	1.6	13	33.0	34	86.4
¾	19	1.9	14	35.6	35	88.9
⅞	22	2.2	15	38.1	36	91.4
1	25	2.5	16	40.6	37	94.0
1¼	32	3.2	17	43.2	38	96.5
1½	38	3.8	18	45.7	39	99.1
1¾	44	4.4	19	48.3	40	101.6
2	51	5.1	20	50.8	41	104.1
2½	64	6.4	21	53.3	42	106.7
3	76	7.6	22	55.9	43	109.2
3½	89	8.9	23	58.4	44	111.8
4	102	10.2	24	61.0	45	114.3
4½	114	11.4	25	63.5	46	116.8
5	127	12.7	26	66.0	47	119.4
6	152	15.2	27	68.6	48	121.9
7	178	17.8	28	71.1	49	124.5
8	203	20.3	29	73.7	50	127.0

YARDS TO METRES

YARDS	METRES	YARDS	METRES	YARDS	METRES	YARDS	METRES	YARDS	METRES
⅛	0.11	2⅛	1.94	4⅛	3.77	6⅛	5.60	8⅛	7.43
¼	0.23	2¼	2.06	4¼	3.89	6¼	5.72	8¼	7.54
⅜	0.34	2⅜	2.17	4⅜	4.00	6⅜	5.83	8⅜	7.66
½	0.46	2½	2.29	4½	4.11	6½	5.94	8½	7.77
⅝	0.57	2⅝	2.40	4⅝	4.23	6⅝	6.06	8⅝	7.89
¾	0.69	2¾	2.51	4¾	4.34	6¾	6.17	8¾	8.00
⅞	0.80	2⅞	2.63	4⅞	4.46	6⅞	6.29	8⅞	8.12
1	0.91	3	2.74	5	4.57	7	6.40	9	8.23
1⅛	1.03	3⅛	2.86	5⅛	4.69	7⅛	6.52	9⅛	8.34
1¼	1.14	3¼	2.97	5¼	4.80	7¼	6.63	9¼	8.46
1⅜	1.26	3⅜	3.09	5⅜	4.91	7⅜	6.74	9⅜	8.57
1½	1.37	3½	3.20	5½	5.03	7½	6.86	9½	8.69
1⅝	1.49	3⅝	3.31	5⅝	5.14	7⅝	6.97	9⅝	8.80
1¾	1.60	3¾	3.43	5¾	5.26	7¾	7.09	9¾	8.92
1⅞	1.71	3⅞	3.54	5⅞	5.37	7⅞	7.20	9⅞	9.03
2	1.83	4	3.66	6	5.49	8	7.32	10	9.14

Index

Marbleized Planter Box